Why Do Teachers Need to Know about Diverse Learning Needs?

PERSONAL, SOCIAL AND EMOTIONAL PERSPECTIVES FOR EDUCATORS

Series Editor: Sue Soan, Canterbury Christ Church University, UK

Why Do Teachers Need to Know about Child Development? Strengthening Professional Identity and Well-Being, edited by Daryl Maisey and Verity Campbell-Barr

Why Do Teachers Need to Know about Diverse Learning Needs? Strengthening Professional Identity and Well-Being, edited by Sue Soan

Why Do Teachers Need to Know about Psychology? Strengthening Professional Identity and Well-Being, edited by Jeremy Monsen, Lisa Marks Woolfson and James Boyle

Other titles available from Bloomsbury

Reflective Teaching in Early Education, Jennifer Colwell and Amanda Ince with Helen Bradford, Helen Edwards, Julian Grenier, Eleanor Kitto, Eunice Lumsden, Catriona McDonald, Juliet Mickelburgh, Mary Moloney, Sheila Nutkins, Ioanna Palaiologou, Deborah Price and Rebecca Swindells

Readings for Reflective Teaching in Early Education, edited by Jennifer Colwell and Andrew Pollard

Reflective Teaching in Schools, Andrew Pollard with Pete Dudley, Steve Higgins, Kristine Black-Hawkins, Gabrielle Cliff Hodges, Mary James, Sue Swaffield, Mandy Swann, Mark Winterbottom, Mary Anne Wolpert and Holly Linklater

Readings for Reflective Teaching in Schools, edited by Andrew Pollard

Reflective Teaching in Further, Adult and Vocational Education, Margaret Gregson and Sam Duncan with Kevin Brosnan, Jay Derrick, Gary Husband, Lawrence Nixon, Trish Spedding, Rachel Stubley and Robin Webber-Jones

Reading for Reflective Teaching in Further, Adult and Vocational Education, Margaret Gregson, Lawrence Nixon, Andrew Pollard and Trish Spedding

Reflective Teaching in Higher Education, Paul Ashwin with David Boud, Susanna Calkins, Kelly Coate, Fiona Hallett, Gregory Light, Kathy Luckett, Jan McArthur, Iain McLaren, Monica McLean, Velda McCune, Katarina Mårtensson and Michelle Tooher

Why Do Teachers Need to Know about Diverse Learning Needs?

Strengthening Professional Identity and Well-Being

Edited by Sue Soan

BLOOMSBURY ACADEMIC
LONDON • NEW YORK • OXFORD • NEW DELHI • SYDNEY

BLOOMSBURY ACADEMIC
Bloomsbury Publishing Plc
50 Bedford Square, London, WC1B 3DP, UK
1385 Broadway, New York, NY 10018, USA
29 Earlsfort Terrace, Dublin 2, Ireland

BLOOMSBURY, BLOOMSBURY ACADEMIC and the Diana logo are
trademarks of Bloomsbury Publishing Plc

First published in Great Britain 2021

Cover design by Charlotte James
Cover image © naqiewei/ iStock

A catalogue record for this book is available from the British Library.

Library of Congress Cataloging-in-Publication Data
Names: Soan, Sue, editor.
Title: Why Do Teachers Need to Know about Diverse Learning Needs?: Strengthening
Professional Identity and Well-Being / Edited by Sue Soan.
Description: London; New York: Bloomsbury Academic, 2021.|
Series: Personal, social and emotional perspectives for educators | Includes bibliographical
references and index.
Identifiers: LCCN 2020036943 (print) | LCCN 2020036944 (ebook) | ISBN 9781350083196
(hardback) | ISBN 9781350083189 (paperback) | ISBN 9781350083202 (epub) | ISBN
9781350083219 (ebook)
Subjects: LCSH: Inclusive education. | Learning disabled children. | Teacher-student relationships.
Classification: LCC LC1200 .W58 2021 (print) | LCC LC1200 (ebook) | DDC 371.9/046–dc23
LC record available at https://lccn.loc.gov/2020036943
LC ebook record available at https://lccn.loc.gov/2020036944

ISBN: HB: 978-1-3500-8319-6
        PB: 978-1-3500-8318-9
        ePDF: 978-1-3500-8321-9
        ePUB: 978-1-3500-8320-2

Series: Personal, Social and Emotional Perspectives for Educators

Typeset by Integra Software Services Pvt. Ltd.
Printed and bound in Great Britain

To find out more about our authors and books visit www.bloomsbury.com
and sign up for our newsletters.

Grace and Poppy
My sunshine
Follow your hopes and dreams

Contents

Figures

Tables

Series Editor's Preface

The textbooks in the *Personal, Social and Emotional Perspective for Educators* series are explicitly designed to support teachers in establishing and developing an holistic understanding of a teacher's role and responsibilities in the twenty-first century. They specifically aim to help trainee, beginning and experienced teachers gain both confidence and knowledge in their professional role working with pupils from the early years through to university entrance. Each book asks the question '*Why do teachers need to know about … '* and is focused on a different area of pedagogy crucial for modern-day teaching practice, providing a breadth of perspectives about teaching and learning. Importantly, in conjunction with this they provide practice examples and searching questions which challenge readers to consider their own views, beliefs and values, on child development, special, able and talented and dual exceptionality and psychology. This innovative book series gives teachers the opportunity and space to develop an enhanced understanding of their role and the professional self.

Recognizing the importance of both practice and theory every chapter is co-authored by a teacher practitioner from various stages of schooling and an education academic, enabling real-life cases from around the world to be discussed alongside theoretical and research-based studies. Although chapter titles will differ between the books the same topics of discussion will be critically explored in most cases. These will consider the importance of the professional self, health and well-being, outdoor education, technology, listening to pupils and reflective practice.

My editorial colleagues and I hope this book series will provide you with a clear sense of the significance and value of the teacher's role and the art of inclusive teaching for all pupils. Teaching is without doubt a demanding and all-encompassing profession, but with resilience and a continuing willingness to learn and adapt, it is one of the most rewarding.

Dr Sue Soan
Series Editor

Series Editor's Introduction to the *Personal, Social and Emotional Perspectives for Educators* Series

This is a textbook trilogy which will help trainee, beginning and experienced teachers gain confidence and knowledge in working with pupils aged two through to nineteen (and perhaps even beyond). Unlike other texts it provides teachers with the opportunity to consider their practice not only from the perspective of strategies or interventions used and curricula engaged with, but also through a holistic examination of their professional role and responsibilities.

The titles of the book series *Personal, Social and Emotional Perspectives for Educators* are:

> *Why Do Teachers Need to Know about Child Development?*
> *Why Do Teachers Need to Know about Diverse Learning Needs?*
> *Why Do Teachers Need to Know about Psychology?*

The series aims to enable every teacher to see why and how it is essential they recognize their own personal, social and emotional responsibilities when educating their pupils. It is for this reason the titles of each book ask a question. The editors consider it is important for all teachers to consistently ask the question 'why?' from their own personal perspective as well as from a professional perspective. Without this ongoing reflection and reflexivity, practice can become 'stale' and views 'fixed'. Twenty-first century life is not static, but constantly changing and throwing humankind unexpected challenges, requiring professionals and leaders to be flexible, well-informed change agents and open to new knowledge. But, of course, it is no use asking 'why?' if the 'how' and 'what' are neglected because without a focus on these type of questions as well teachers will not know what needs to change or how to change them. Thus, throughout the series, answers to the 'why?' questions are given through exploration of the 'what and how', enabling teachers the opportunity to develop a deep understanding of how they can enhance their practice and as a consequence maintain motivation and enhance their resilience and expertise.

The books are written with an international audience in mind and hope to support all teachers around the world whatever their context or pupil age group. The decision was made that the term 'pupil' would be used to try and avoid confusion between school pupils and teacher trainees or students. This generic term also facilitated avoiding the often, artificial boundaries teachers and other educators put around practice for different age groups. All children and young people, whatever their age, learning, social or emotional needs are therefore called pupils. It is hoped that no one is offended by this decision and if so, that was not the intention. All actual names used in chapters have been altered to maintain anonymity unless specific written agreement has been obtained stating that their name or the name of an institution can be used. Of course, language has not been altered in any quotations, in the Window on research or Case studies and 'child' or 'children' is used when parental perspectives are offered.

Whichever book in the series is picked up first, readers will find that all authors examine, through the subject content, what it means to be a 'teacher'. They consider not only aspects such as the professional self, but also the role of reflection and reflexivity in developing an understanding of the self and the day-to-day experiences in teaching. For clarity, *reflection* is defined in the books as the action of personal purposeful thinking about education to improve professional practice. *Reflexivity* involves 'question[ing] our own attitudes, theories-in-use, values, assumptions, prejudices and habitual actions; to understand our complex roles in relation to others' (Bolton and Delderfield, 2018:10 in Chapter 8 of *Why Do Teachers Need to Know about Diverse Learning Needs?*). As Codina and Fordham (2021:120, in Soan, 2021:119-136) state 'a teacher's reflexive awareness should therefore shape their in-action reflections; i.e. the in the moment choices teachers make concerning interactions with others (colleagues, parents, children)'.

Recognizing the significance of connecting theory to practice and vice versa, each chapter (with the exception of Chapter 1 in *Why Do Teachers Need to Know about Diverse Learning Needs?*) is co-written by a teacher practitioner and an education academic. This enables the welding together of practice experience and knowledge, and theoretical and research evidence, rather than just providing a passing glance from one arena to the other.

Finally, it is anticipated that these books will provide teachers at all stages of their professional career with the information and challenge required for them to see the significance and value of the teacher role and the art of teaching for all pupils whatever their learning or developmental needs. Humankind needs teachers now more than ever who can motivate, capture their pupils' interests and abilities, and challenge them to always ask questions and seek answers. Teaching can be without doubt the most fulfilling profession when fully understood, and it is suggested that as a natural consequence of this every pupil then becomes inclusively taught, valued and nurtured.

Dr Sue Soan
Series Editor

Using This Book

Each book follows a similar structure. Due to its professional parameters and distinctive focus, *Why Do Teachers Need to Know about Psychology?* considers technology and learning environments within chapters rather than having specific chapters on these topics. Each chapter is designed to critically explore different subject areas. These are reflected across the trilogy and are considered important to professional development today and include:

- The professional self
- Health and well-being
- The learning environment
- Technology
- Listening
- Professional relationships and collaboration
- Resilience, reflection, reflexivity
- The role of the teacher

Within each chapter

Each chapter includes a number of features to make connections between theory and practice explicit and alive, drawing on experiences and research from a range of settings:

 Case studies

 Window on research

 Window on practice
(Why do Teachers Need to Know
About Child Development?)

 Reflective questions

 Reflexive questions

Each chapter ends with an Annotated bibliography.

At the end of the book

In order to also support busy educators, trainees and teachers, all of the references, whilst placed together towards the end of the book, are listed in chapter order.

Editor

Sue Soan

Sue is a university lecturer, supervising doctoral students on research relating to special educational needs. She is also an educational adviser for fostering organizations and schools and undertakes clinical supervision with school leaders. Prior to 2003 Sue taught in nursery settings, primary mainstream and special schools for over twenty-five years, as a classroom teacher, a subject coordinator (mathematics), a special educational need's coordinator (SENCO) and Senior Leader. Her doctoral thesis (2013) explored the education provision of Looked after Children who had experienced early-life abuse and neglect. Her research interests include the SENCO role, motor and coordination development, multi-professional working, Looked after Children, autism and clinical supervision. As an authority in her field, she has published in peer-reviewed journals and presented her research at national and international conferences. Sue is a school governor at a mainstream primary school and is a Trustee of a national SEN organization.

Contributors

Alan Bainbridge

Alan Bainbridge is a Chartered Psychologist, Doctor of Clinical Science and Senior Lecturer in Education at Canterbury Christ Church University, UK, having previously taught in secondary schools for eighteen years. He is interested in the contested space between psychoanalytic thought and practices to education in its widest sense and is a co-coordinator of the European Society for Research on the Education of Adults Life History and Biography Network. He has written on how educational professionals develop their professional practice, including the monograph 'Becoming an Education Professional' (2015). He is currently exploring the fetish in education and how human learning and the 'natural world' are interconnected. Alan has recently used narrative and biographical techniques to research the motivators and barriers towards a community engagement project and the attitude of individuals towards the re-introduction of native wild carnivores. He uses his experience as a UKCP-registered psychoanalytic psychotherapist to inform his research and as such works qualitatively to seek to provide opportunities and spaces where participants can provide rich contextual data of their life experiences. It is from this perspective that Alan has drawn on to develop the successful ongoing research project on Support and Supervision in Education.

Christian Couper

Christian is a primary school principal leading and teaching in a small rural school in Canterbury, New Zealand. Christian works with a team of creative educators who seek ways to personalize the learning experience for pupils and their families. Christian is married to Maria, also an experienced teacher, with two daughters nearing the end of their school careers. He is often reminded by these wise women at home that the true role of a teacher is to understand the unique needs of each person and to enable them to be agents in their own learning. In an attempt to live a balanced life, Christian enjoys trail runs in the wild places of New Zealand with the family dog and is currently testing his own collaborative skills with his Swim-Run partner in the open waters of the South Island.

Geraldene Codina

Geraldene is a Senior Lecturer at the University of Derby, UK. She is the programme leader for the MA Inclusion and Special Educational Needs and Disabilities and the National Award for SENCOs. As part of her role in higher education she has worked with the Department for Education, nasen and number of Local Authorities. Geraldene is currently the Chair of the Derby Opportunity Area SEND Project Management Group.

Teresa Dowling

Following a ten-year career as a Mainstream Class Teacher, Teresa completed her MA in Inclusion and Institutional Development, specializing in Autism Spectrum Disorder (ASD). Teresa then worked in, and led, a large Specialist Resource Provision, in Kent, for children, with an Education, Health and Care plan and primary need of ASD. During this time, as the Provision's SENCO, she dealt with all Annual Reviews and EHC plan provision and acquired the National Award for SENCO. Most recently, Teresa began working for a Local Authority providing specialist expertise in supporting the monitoring, evaluation and development of SEN provision within mainstream schools.

Alison Ekins

Alison Ekins is a Senior Lecturer in Education at Canterbury Christ Church University, UK, and also works as Director of SEN within an Academy Trust of eight primary and secondary schools. Alison's particular areas of interest and expertise are in the fields of Special Educational Needs and Inclusion, having completed a Doctorate of Education focusing on exploring the individual experiences of how schools have developed and understand inclusive practices, and having worked in schools for over twenty years supporting children, families and staff to understand and positively manage the challenges of special educational needs and inclusive practices.

Alison has also worked closely with colleagues from the Health Faculty at Canterbury Christ Church University to research and publish about the experience of mainstream teachers in coping with meeting the needs of children with life-limiting conditions, and processes to support mainstream teachers to better understand the challenges and issues with this in order to put in place proactive support for children, their families and the wider school community.

Understanding the emotional impact of the work that practitioners undertake in schools is at the heart of the research and work that Alison undertakes and has written about.

Nicola Elson

Nicola Elson is a Researcher at the University of Kent and an Associate Lecturer at Canterbury Christ Church University, UK. She has over twenty years' experience teaching and working in senior leadership roles in a number of schools including six special schools for pupils with autism, profound and multiple learning difficulties, sensory and physical impairments. She is currently studying for her PhD in the field of Special Educational Needs and Disability and has published on transitioning from special schools as well as supporting relationships for people with learning disabilities.

Jon Fordham

Jon has been a headteacher in Derby city, UK, for seven years. He is a local leader of education and has been involved in research projects with Derby University, UK, for over four years. He is a facilitator for Inspiring Leaders NPQ programmes and has led training on metacognition (children and adults), leadership and school improvement. As part of his partnership work, he has written a number of research papers including co-authoring a book on evidence-based teaching.

Lorna Hughes

Lorna Hughes is a Senior Lecturer in Special Educational Needs and Inclusion in the Faculty of Education at Canterbury Christ Church University, UK. Her research interests include multi-agency working and the impact of collaborative practices for the learner as well as how policy translates into practice in real-world settings. Recent publications include 'Skilling up for health and well-being – the professional development challenge' (2016). Her PhD studies focus on the role of parents and schools in the co-production of statutory assessment plans for children with more complex needs.

Conor Mc Guckin

Conor Mc Guckin is Assistant Professor of Educational Psychology in the School of Education at Trinity College Dublin, Ireland. Conor convenes the Inclusion in Education and Society Research Group and is the founding editor of the International Journal of Inclusion in Education and Society. Conor's research interests include psychology applied to educational policy and practices, bully/victim problems among children and adults, and special and inclusive education. Conor is an Associate Fellow of both the British Psychological Society (BPS) and the Psychological Society of Ireland (PSI). Conor is a Chartered Psychologist with both the BPS and the PSI and is a Chartered Scientist with the UK Science Council.

Joy Mower

Joy is a Senior Lecturer at Canterbury Christ Church University, UK, teaching across Primary ITE programme. Her areas of interest and expertise are English and Art and Design. She worked for the BBC for twenty years before undertaking a PGCE at Canterbury Christ Church University and then an MA in Enabling learning, Inclusion and Institutional development, focusing on special educational needs, particularly language and literacy difficulties. She has experience of working as a class teacher and leading literacy across a large primary school with specialist provision for speech, language and communication need. Joy has made five trips to Palestine to work with colleagues there as the English consultant in a Canterbury Christ Church University team working collaboratively with universities in Palestine, within the World Bank–funded Teacher Education Improvement Project. This project won the 2018 Times Higher Education International Impact Award. Joy has also provided teachers' continuing professional development courses for Kent County Council. She is currently studying for a PhD exploring children and teachers understanding of drawing as an alternative mode of meaning-making in children's classroom text-making.

Carol-Ann O'Síoráin

Carol-Ann is a Lecturer in Education in the School of Education, Hibernia College, Ireland. Carol-Ann's research interests are in the areas of special and inclusive pedagogy, supporting the education of learners with intellectual and neuro-developmental difference, the voice and role of parents in education, and the role of play and playfulness in advancing communication and access to learning. Carol-Ann has held many roles in relation to Special Education and Early Childhood, notably as advisor to government initiatives and a President of the Irish Association of Teachers in Special Education. She is actively engaged in the Inclusion in Education and Society Research (IES) Group in the School of Education Trinity College, Dublin. She is current chair of The Children's Research Network Early childhood Special Interest Group and she is a founding member of the Researching Early Childhood Education Collaborative (RECEC) with Professor Nóirín Hayes.

John-Paul Riordan

John is a Senior Lecturer in Education at Canterbury Christ Church University, UK. His PhD in 2014 was in science education (conceptual change pedagogy). He taught secondary school science (specializing in physics) from 1999 to 2016. He worked full-time in mainstream schools for ten years and then taught for seven years in a special school for children with complex needs. He is a Makaton Tutor (Canterbury Christ Church University is the first in the world to become Makaton-Friendly). He teaches on undergraduate and postgraduate programmes, mostly in primary education Initial Teacher Education but also on the MA in SEN and Inclusion. He supervises Master and Doctoral students, specializing in video-based pedagogy analysis and SEN Inclusion.

Mark Roberts

Mark is a Senior Lecturer in Education at Canterbury Christ Church University, UK. He taught secondary English and drama in mainstream schools from 1992 to 1999 before moving to work in a special school for children with physical difficulties and complex medical needs from 1999 to 2019. He worked initially as an English teacher before moving into senior leadership. He continues to work as a governor for a special school and is currently undertaking research with non-verbal children. He teaches on foundation, undergraduate and postgraduate programmes, mostly in primary education Initial Teacher Education with a focus upon SEN and Inclusion.

Acknowledgements

I would like to thank Jeremy Monsen, Lisa Marks Woolfson, Jim Boyle, Verity Campbell-Barr and Daryl Maisey for sharing the writing and editing of this book series with me. It has been a privilege working with you. I would also wish to thank all of the authors who have contributed chapters to this book for their positivity, patience and support. Last, but not least, I would like to thank my family and especially Mark, my husband, for his constant support, love, encouragement and honesty.

Abbreviations

AAC	Augmentative and Alternative Communication
AIDS	Acquired immunodeficiency syndrome
AfA	Achievement for All
AGT	Able, Gifted and Talented
AR	Augmented Reality
ASC	Autism Spectrum Condition
ASD	Autism Spectrum Disorder
BSL	British Sign Language
ChYPMHS	Children's and Young People Mental Health Services
CPD	Continuing Professional Development
CQC	Care Quality Commission
CRPD	Convention on the Rights of Persons with Disabilities
DfE	Department of Education
DMD	Duchenne Muscular Dystrophy
DME	Dual and/or Multiple Exceptionalities
DoH	Department of Health
EADSNE	European Agency for Development in Special Needs Education
EP	Educational Psychologist
EY	Early Years
G&T	Gifted and Talented
GT	Gifted and Talented
HIV	human immunodeficiency virus
HoC	House of Commons
HPL	High Potential Learning
ICT	Information and Communication Technology
ITE	Initial Teacher Education
LAC	Looked after Child (by the State)
LD	Learning Difficulties
NAO	National Audit Office
NQT	Newly Qualified Teacher
OECD	Organization for Economic Co-operation and Development
Ofsted	Office for Standards in Education

OHCHR	Office of the High Commissioner for Human Rights
OT	Occupational Therapist
PBIS	Positive Behaviour Interventions and Support
PECs	Picture Exchange Communications System
PhET	Physics Education Technology
PPEO	Policy, Practice (provision), Experiences, and Outcomes
Primary School	Equivalent to Elementary School in the United States, covering ages of about five to ten
PRU	Pupil Referral Unit
SALT	Speech and Language Therapist
SAMR	Substitution, Augmentation, Modification and Redefinition
SDG	Sustainable Development Goals
Secondary School	Equivalent to Junior High and High School in the United States, covering ages roughly eleven to eighteen years
SETT	Student Environment Tasks Tools
SEMH	Social, Emotional and Mental Health
SEN	Special Educational Needs
SENCO	Special Educational Needs Coordinator
SEND	Special Educational Needs and Disabilities
SLCD	Speech, Language and/or Communication Difficulties
SNA	Special Need Assistant
SpLD	Specific Learning Difficulty
SRP	Specialist Resource Provision
TA	Teaching Assistant
TEACCH	Teaching, Expanding, Appreciating, Collaborating and Cooperating, and Holistic
UD	Universal Design
UDL	Universal Design Learning
UN	United Nations
UNCRC	UN Convention on the Rights of the Child
UNESCO	United Nations Educational, Scientific and Cultural Organization
UNICEF	United Nations International Children's Emergency Fund
VLL	Virtual Learning Lab
VOCA	Voice Output Communication Aid
VR	Virtual reality
WHO	World Health Organization

1

Setting the Context

Sue Soan

Introduction

This first chapter briefly outlines the key conversations and debates that teachers will be able to engage with when working with pupils with diverse learning needs. First, globalization of learning will be explored, followed by a case study reminding us that global does not mean forgetting about individual pupil need. Teaching inclusively is then introduced, before moving on to discuss pupil learning needs, special educational needs and 'gifts and talents'. Finally, the contents of each chapter in this volume are described for you.

Globalization of learning

The design and wide distribution of the internet has meant people across the world have in recent years gained greater personal connectivity via rapid distribution of cellular networks and mini-satellites. This ever-evolving technological change must influence our understanding of the world; of work, play and learning. In the past the purpose of teaching and intended learning was to train a future workforce for known employment in the near future. Subjects and curriculums were designed to provide a graduated skills development for a known end job.

More recent global reforms are changing educational curriculums to a lesser or greater degree in countries, with greater focus on growing competencies for lifelong learning, for ongoing adaptation and sustainability of employment options that can evolve with whatever the future economies of the world may depend on. Change occurs fast and is of course affected by the actions of humans, intended and unintended, as we have found out with the 2020 pandemic and climate change. Hence whilst individual home and virtual schooling can positively support learning, it cannot provide a level of consistency, inclusion and scale for a government, or governance philosophy. It is therefore considered that schools will remain relevant for state education, but the role and responsibilities of teachers will most likely need to be more fluid and adaptive with collaboration as a key element required to enable effective responses to rapidly changing agendas and personal and professional well-being.

Schwartz et al. (2019) predict that a world of human-machine collaboration will emerge quickly and that it is skills of problem-solving, communication, listening, interpretation and design that will be required to 'get the work done' and thus need to be nurtured and valued in school education. Little did we know that the coronavirus pandemic in 2020 would make this prediction a reality so quickly.

Cognizant of fast developing markets, schools, through their teachers and with their pupils, are making changes to curriculums to refocus on developing easily transferable skill sets and capacities to continue learning beyond the schools that will support the evolution of this new workforce. All of this is likely to influence the role and responsibilities of a teacher and more specifically for this volume how pupils' differences and strengths are viewed. This is the global and national influence on schools and teachers, but of course the role of a teacher incorporates not only meeting global and national aspirations, but local and individual pupil ones as well. The following case study illustrates an example of a teacher meeting the social and emotional needs of one pupil impacting significantly on the pupil's experiences and life chances. Teaching is a complex profession, but one I have personally felt a privilege to be part of: being trusted to help educate our future generations.

Case study: Saying goodbye

Country: UK

Age group: 9 years

Setting: A car journey

Participants involved: Sue and Graham[1], one of her pupils – leaving a residential school

The case

When thinking about why teachers need to know about individual pupils' learning needs, from those who have complex and life-limiting medical needs to those who are highly academically able or talented, Sue recalled a very sad journey, but one in which the pupil portrayed hope and resilience.

Graham had been attending a special residential home (and school) for children and young people who had experienced severe abuse or trauma. Some of the pupils attended mainstream schools and were successful learners; others, like Graham, had previously not been able to attend school for a couple of years and went to the school on site. It took a long time for

[1] Not his real name.

Graham to feel safe enough to build trust in the teachers and to accept support. Although he was an intuitive and able mathematician he struggled with literacy and was eventually found to have dyslexia. Responding to Graham's need to 'belong', to have something of his own, Sue decided to support his literacy development with an intervention programme which was completely his own – an expensive resource, but she felt it was vital for his emotional as well as his learning needs. Progress accelerated to everyone's delight (through collaborative working) – but this was short-lived, as his home local authority decided that academically he had made so much progress he could return to his home authority to live and attend a mainstream school. On being told this, Graham's behaviour immediately regressed, resulting finally in the residential provision 'giving notice' to his home local authority due to his high level of aggression and violence – and fears that he could not be kept safe.

Sue was asked to travel in the car with Graham on the journey back to his home authority, because he had never attacked her, and they got on well. The journey was about four hours long. Emotions were quite raw and the sadness of having to say goodbye in such circumstances was palpable for all sharing the journey. School matters were discussed along the way and one time after a period of silence Graham turned to Sue clutching the literacy resource he had been given all those many months ago and said smiling: 'Don't worry Sue, I will keep working through my tasks every day. I won't forget, I want to keep learning to read and write.' Somehow Sue managed to respond saying that she would not expect anything less …. Sue can still remember the date that Graham left.

Outcome

Graham's teenage years were not straightforward, but Sue later heard that he had got a job, was doing well and was making a positive life for himself. She also recognized that the decisions made by the adults commissioning the service were not pupil-focused, but were responding predominately to short-time economic and political pressures, forgetting that their decisions could have consequences for Graham's whole life.

What we can learn

This extract shows how Sue undertook her teaching and learning responsibilities seriously as evidenced by Graham's academic progress. But there was much Sue had to consider, plan and evaluate to enable that success, over and above implementing that required for regular pupils. Unravelling the complexities of Graham's needs, it can be seen he had what is currently termed 'Dual and Multiple Exceptionalities (DME)' as he had high mathematical ability, and a special educational need (dyslexia), combined with attachment and experiences of severe abuse (physical and emotional). He was also a 'Looked after Child' (a child living outside of his family home) and therefore the Local Authority was responsible for his care and well-being. In this one situation the following elements of a teacher's role can be identified:

- The importance of relationships
- Pupil-centred holistic approach
- Knowledge of DME (Special and Able education)
- Collaboration skills and abilities
- A positive personal and professional attitude towards difference and Looked after Children
- An understanding of the impact of abuse on the cognitive, emotional and social life of a pupil
- The priorities of a Local Authority
- A pupil's life opportunities.

Reflective questions

1. What skills, attitudes and knowledge do you think teachers need to demonstrate to teach pupils with special, able, gifted and talented educational needs?
2. If Graham arrived in your class, would you have thought of his holistic and individual needs before introducing intervention programmes or requesting assessments?

Reflexive question

Why did you become a teacher?

Becoming a teacher for ALL pupils: Inclusion

There are a number of views about what encourages a person to become a teacher. Some will become a teacher because it is what the 'family do' and some see the profession as a vocation, whilst in England it has also been said 'If you can't do anything else – teach'. Equally varied are thoughts about what makes a competent or great teacher with views varying about the importance of subject knowledge, good management/behaviour skills and the wish to make a difference. The reality however is not linear, but complicated and multifaceted with impactful government directives, funding and resources issues all playing a role in what and how a teacher teaches.

Arguably though international education policy has for a number of decades been moving towards one of inclusive education with the role of the teacher at the foreground of managing and achieving this, forging a route through all the complexities that this requires. This internationally accepted inclusive education viewpoint can best be understood through the Dakar Agreement and its Framework for Action for an 'Education for All'. A lengthy and broad action plan it distinctly recognizes the vital role teachers need to play to enable such work to be achieved. It says:

> Teachers are essential players in promoting quality education, whether in schools or in more flexible community- based programmes; they are advocates for, and catalysts of, change. No education reform is likely to succeed without the active participation and ownership of teachers.
>
> (UNESCO, 2000, pp. 20, 69)

It continues by emphasizing that 'teachers must also accept their professional responsibilities and be accountable to both learners and communities' (UNESCO, 2000, pp. 20, 69), the underlined words of which the most recent English SEND code of practice: 0–25 (DfE and DoH, 2015) also adopted. Importantly, the 'Education for All' title is also demonstrated in the following section highlighting the thought that all teachers need to be able to work with and provide for the educational needs of all their pupils:

> Teachers must be able to understand diversity in learning styles and in the physical and intellectual development of students, and to create stimulating, participatory learning environments.
>
> (UNESCO, 2000, pp. 20–1:70)

But what knowledge, interpersonal and professional skills, and ongoing continuing training and development do teachers need in order for them to manage the role and the responsibilities alongside ensuring their own professional values and beliefs and well-being are maintained?

Reflective questions

1. Do you think you can be or are a teacher who works effectively with all pupils who have a diverse learning need, often termed as special, able, gifted or talented?
2. What factors influence your answer to this question?

Meeting pupil need

It is suggested that every pupil will at some point in their school education experience a time when they find learning more difficult than other pupils, resulting in learning plateauing or not progressing as 'expected' even if they are not formally labelled as requiring a special educational needs (SEN) intervention. Such need might be identified in a specific area of a curriculum programme, a subject itself or seen to be a mental health, physical, emotional or social difficulty.

Likewise, pupils with high ability or specific talents in one or more subjects or fields of study may well find they need additional and different intervention or provision to their peers either constantly during their school life or at various points in their education. Often neglected or unobserved, these needs can have equal if not more impact on the long-term outcomes of these pupils. Whilst some may find their way successfully through the maze towards adulthood, many necessitate teachers to both recognize their diverse and complex needs and then remove the barriers to their learning.

Of course, to achieve what can be called 'population schooling', a standard 'national' curriculum is a reasonable response with development and progress measures for the 'typical' pupil expected detailed. One view is that such a curriculum could be considered the 'core' or typical curriculum, supporting the assumption to be made that enable teachers to work flexibly, allowing a whole school or provision approach to meet the needs of their community.

> ### Reflective question
> Reflect on all of the discussions above and think how you view inclusive education and how your school or setting views inclusion.

What is a special educational need (SEN)?

Although the terms used throughout the world continue to differ, the pupils who are referred to with this term or label are those who do not, for a variety of reasons, manage to meet the expected levels of academic progress. It is quite likely that pupils with behavioural needs, sensory issues or difficulties in socializing or understanding social 'rules' within a regular mainstream classroom will also be identified under this 'umbrella' term. Some nations and countries use for example 'additional' or 'inclusive' instead of 'special', but it is considered here that whatever the language used, the pupil group would be the same or at least similar. There is not room in this book to discuss the history and development of special educational needs education in detail, but Figure 1.1 provides a brief overview showing the conception and evolution of 'special educational needs' in England. Despite such immense legislative journeys as described in Figure 1.1, I posit that professionals, parents and the pupils themselves continue to believe current systems are still failing large numbers of pupils with SEN even though the majority of people would agree with the statement that 'all children deserve a good education, with staff in schools giving them the confidence, self-belief and teaching that they need to fulfil their potential' (DfE, 2011, p. 65).

The term 'special educational needs' was adopted in UK legislation (Department of Education and Science, 1981) following the publication of the Warnock Report (HMSO, 1978) and has ever since influenced the direction of policy and practice. Through its creation Mary Warnock and colleagues attempted to move terminology (and perhaps mindsets also) from a medical model of disability to a social or psycho-social model. It also introduced 'integration' into mainstream schools challenging segregation provision and forcing a noticeable shift in ideology from segregation to integration. Despite this it was not until the 1993 Education Act (part III) that legislation for a Code of Practice was passed leading to its publication in 1994 (DfE, 1994).

Two further Codes of Practice have been introduced by different governments (DfE and DoH, 2014, 2015; DfES, 2001) since the original one, in response to changing political, economic and social demands. Whilst the 'how' to identify, assess, record and evaluate has changed in each code, the term 'SEN' for school-aged children has remained the same with just slight adjustments in age groups and use of language since 1994:

'xiii. A child or young person has SEN if they have a learning difficulty or disability which calls for special educational provision to be made for him or her.

xiv. A child of compulsory school age or a young person has a learning difficulty or disability if he or she:

- has a significantly greater difficulty in learning than the majority of others of the same age, or
- has a disability which prevents or hinders him or her from making use of facilities of a kind generally provided for others of the same age in mainstream schools or post-16 institutions' (DfE and DoH, 2015, pp. 15–16).

The role and responsibilities of teachers (as well as others) have been strengthened and increased with regards to working with pupils with SEN from the first to the current code of practice with words such as 'must' and 'should' being used in statements to infer expected compliance. The SEND code of practice (DfE and DoH, 2015, p. 99, 6.36 and 6.37) says:

'Teachers are responsible and accountable for the progress and development of the pupils in their class, including where pupils access support from teaching assistants or specialist staff (6.36).

High quality teaching, differentiated for individual pupils, is the first step in responding to pupils who have or may have SEN. Additional intervention and support cannot compensate for a lack of good quality teaching. Schools should regularly and carefully review the quality of teaching for all pupils, including those at risk of underachievement. This includes reviewing and, where necessary, improving, teachers' understanding of strategies to identify and support vulnerable pupils and their knowledge of the SEN most frequently encountered (6.37).'

Due to the less than favourable outcomes emerging from practice, the present government of the UK has decided to carry out a further review. This is currently underway (April 2020).

Figure 1.1 A brief overview of 'Special Educational Needs' in England.

What is able, gifted and talented education?

Just like the term 'special educational needs' the language used to describe pupils who are very academically able, have talents in specific fields or have a combination of both special and high ability (Dual, Multiple Exceptionalities (DME)) (e.g. Autism Spectrum Disorders (ASD) or dyslexia) can be seen as unfavourable or even disliked by some. Definitions of 'able, gifted and talented' are often contested and thus it is argued here that following profiles of characteristics, like those offered by Silverman,[2] and Betts and Neihart (1988),[3] might present greater guidance. The characteristics described by Betts and Neihart's profiles are under the headings of: The Successful, The Creative, The Dual or Multiple Exceptional, The Autonomous, The Underground and The At-Risk. Each country and organization unsurprisingly have their own language for pupils with these needs and another phrase used is 'High Potential Learners' (HPL)[4]. Up until a decade ago the UK had a national programme for developing practice for pupils who were able and/or talented, but with the change of government and the rise of austerity the programme ended. Whilst there is an assumption that schools will always ensure every pupil achieves their potential there is little evidence of emphasis placed on any direct thinking for the needs of these pupils across all schools. The latest Ofsted framework (Ofsted, 2019, pp. 9, 26) (the Inspection organization) appears to only specifically mention pupils with high needs in one place:

---

[2] https://www.spart5.net/cms/lib07/SC01000802/Centricity/Domain/491/Characteristics_Scale.pdf
[3] https://www.potentialplusuk.org/index.php/profiles-of-children-with-hlp/
[4] https://www.potentialplusuk.org/index.php/families/getting-your-child-best-support/

Inspectors will make a judgement on the quality of education by evaluating the extent to which: Intent v leaders take on or construct a curriculum that is ambitious and designed to give all learners, particularly the most disadvantaged and those with special educational needs and/or disabilities (SEND) or high needs, the knowledge and cultural capital they need to succeed in life.

As you can see it is mentioned alongside all other labels of additional need in this document. This is to some extent understandable because if a pupil with 'high need' or 'high learning potential' does not feel well supported or challenged appropriately they may display similar characteristics as seen in pupils with other forms of additional need such as:

- struggling to fit in with their peers,
- losing the motivation to learn,
- questioning authority and demonstrating challenging behaviour,
- overly anxious or impatient,
- lacking self-esteem,
- refusing to go to school or truanting, experiencing bullying,
- not making learning progress.

These can sometimes lead to a 'misdiagnosis' of need and consequently unhappy pupils and families who perhaps find it difficult to find their 'place' in school or the world.

Reflective questions

1. Do you recognize these descriptions and considerations of SEND and Able, Gifted and Talented educational needs?
2. Are they helpful in your daily teaching, planning, assessment and evaluation of progress?

Reflexive questions

1. Do you have an internal positive or negative response to these terms?
2. If so, why do you think this is the case?

This book

This book shares the experience and knowledge of practitioners and academics from across and beyond the field of education. It is all about knowing the pupils you teach, and yourself, a teacher. It does not provide prescriptive ways of how to teach pupils with special educational needs and disabilities (SEND), high ability/talent or dual and multiple exceptionality (DME), but explains and explores some of the many elements that can be of significant assistance to a teacher's role when teaching pupils with learning differences. Each chapter is co-written by a practitioner and an academic and they present areas of interest with regard to the book's subject matter for you to consider, drawing on their theoretical and experiential expertise. In this manner the authors provide new and, as one author says, 'seasoned' teachers with exciting insights into the many elements that fuse together to create the role of the teacher, helping to develop and evolve learning for all pupils.

Moving on from the overview of special, able, gifted and talented educational needs issues currently, McGuckin and O'Síoráin begin **Chapter 2** by reminding teachers of the importance of reflection and reflexivity and also continuing their professional development throughout their careers. They identify the need for teachers to be aware of their own attitudes and behaviours and to take opportunities to 'stop and stare'. Readers are then introduced to the 'thinking tool' PPEO which aims to help teachers manage workloads through reflecting on the existence of four consistent companions – 'P'olicy, 'P'ractice (provision), 'E'xperiences, and 'O'utcomes alongside 'communications' and 'relationships'. These six elements were found to be key to how special education is provided in Irish schools (Rose et al., 2015). As an overarching structure the authors feel that PPEO help teachers to reflect on their personal and professional responsibilities and the impact that these can have on inclusive practice. Bronfenbrenner's (1989) ecological framework is explored to help teachers understand these influences. Using a brief reference to inclusive education to link the different ideas, the Universal Design (UD) concept is then discussed with specific reference to the needs of pupils with special educational needs.

An important part of the conversation about the professional self is self-care and in the second half of this chapter McGuckin and O'Síoráin provide information for consideration about stress and burnout, partnerships and teacher self-reflections. Finally, case studies and a Window on research, the role of teachers in understanding issues of home-school support and disablist bullying are shared. Through the reflecting on research studies, alongside attending to teachers own personal, social and emotional needs, this chapter reminds teachers that the inclusion of all pupils is everyone's business.

Bainbridge and Ekins write about two key issues in **Chapter 3**. Firstly, they consider the issues relating to the increase in schools of pupils with life-limiting and life- threatening complex medical need. The authors then explore the health, well-being and resilience of teachers and especially those who have leadership responsibilities around SEN, health needs and inclusion for creating an environment where the young people in their charge are cared for. They focus on the importance of caring for the carer, acknowledging that unless individuals can value and look after themselves, it will be less likely that the professional judgements necessary to provide effective care to young people in education settings will be made. Bainbridge and

Ekins provide case study examples of approaches that can be taken to support with these suggestions, and some recommendations for ways that student, newly qualified and experienced teachers can find strategies and support, to mitigate against issues such as fatigue, stress and lack of confidence.

The significance of the learning environment for pupils with individual additional needs is explored in **Chapter 4** by Hughes and Elson. They show how imperative it is that teachers put into place plans and measures to ensure that the environment matches the specific needs of all pupils with special educational needs or the able, gifted and/or talented. Really positively, the chapter considers this from the perspective of pupils at all age phases from early years to post-compulsory education. Themes discussed include the classroom setting, curriculum design, the structure of the school building, the outdoor environment and the wider community linking back to issues discussed in Chapter 2. The authors show how important it is for teachers to consider how they personally, socially and emotionally can help to provide pupils with special educational needs or who are able, gifted and talented with a learning environment which meets their lifelong learning needs.

In the middle of this book is a chapter (**Chapter 5**) about the often challenging but crucial subject of technology. Introduced briefly in Chapter 1 as an area of increasing importance in this century for all teachers, the authors focus on how they can and should be using it to enhance individual pupil's learning and engagement. Riordan and Roberts also indicate ways that the use of technology in schools could develop in the future to support learning. The chapter seeks to help teachers see their role and responsibilities in making their classrooms more technologically inclusive for all pupils, alongside suggesting resources and potential teaching strategies.

Chapter 6 then explores two powerful core professional skills – listening and observation. Mower and Dowling consider how teachers can empower pupils with additional needs, in mainstream and specialized settings, by listening to them and taking their voices into account. The chapter explores how listening can mean creating *explicit* opportunities for pupils to reflect on their perceptions of being a learner in a school which can inform professional decision-making and ongoing practice, as well as being a key *implicit* aspect of good practice within the classroom. The importance of teacher observation and hearing what pupils are saying through their actions is illustrated clearly through a case study of a pupil with autism and a 'Window on research'. The chapter then explains how willingness to hear pupils' voices also requires teachers to listen to all carers with parental responsibilities. Throughout the chapter, the authors consider how teachers' individual thoughts and feelings influence actions and interactions in the classroom and provide opportunities for reflection on these.

From here **Chapter 7** expands on the critical personal skills of a teacher to explain how collaborative working can be supportive when working with pupils with diverse needs within and beyond the physical school's boundaries, if implemented with thought and care. Couper and Soan discuss the complexities of professional collaborative working both between teaching colleagues, and between teachers and professionals from other disciplines. The chapter provides general information and practice examples of what 'working together' really means in a school context in order to achieve positive outcomes for pupils and their families. It provides reasons for working together in schools today, emphasizing its importance for pupils with special educational needs, disabilities and/or those who have complex medical and social needs. It then continues by exploring the benefits of teacher team working and collaboration in schools from the perspective of practitioners in New Zealand. Couper and Soan then explain why all teachers also need to be able to work with professionals from other disciplines. This again is especially vital when working with pupils with a learning difference who frequently need input from a range of professionals from health and social care. Questions such as 'So what is it that enables a teaching team to work together effectively?' and 'How can this collaboration stretch to encompass and value professionals from other fields such as health, policing and social care?' are answered. A case study shows how able pupils need teachers to recognize when and how to gather support from other professionals and colleagues in order for them to engage effectively with learning. Also, findings from a research study discuss joint disciplinary working and indicate how this way of working can have a positive impact on universal support, as well as additional and specific strategies for pupils with additional needs. Throughout, ideas and suggestions to help the successful establishment and maintenance of complex partnerships are explained, once again highlighting how such partnerships can particularly enable and support pupils requiring targeted or specialist intervention and support from professionals other than teachers.

In the penultimate chapter (**Chapter 8**), the authors Codina and Fordham weave together many of the threads already discussed in the preceding chapters showing the importance of understanding interactions between individuals and their environments. The authors consider the moving away from the potentially damaging effects of a 'pull yourself together' mentality, in favour of analysis which contextualizes teacher resilience. They suggest that the desired outcome of this meeting between individual and context is a teacher who experiences professional engagement and growth, commitment, enthusiasm, satisfaction, and well-being and thus is able to act in a personally, socially and emotionally responsible way. The nexus between professional challenge and teacher satisfaction is explored through two case studies which address the inclusion of pupils with special educational needs and/or disability (SEND) and who are considered able, gifted and/or talented.

In **Chapter 9**, Soan and Couper return to the question 'Why do teachers need to know about diverse learning needs?' suggesting that one element that leads a teacher to decide on their career is that they want to make a difference (the 'Why') and to feel they have the confidence and skills to make the right decision for each and every pupil. Political and social drivers within education which challenge teacher's identity, values and beliefs, possibly resulting in internal conflict between personal and professional values, are discussed. The authors explore how fulfilling one important aspect of their role, the performance measurement of pupils (and frequently the teacher through inspection), can be a real challenge for teachers who want to put into practice what they consider is best for pupils with special or high ability needs, for example, but conflicts with system requirements. Further professional dilemmas such as the increased marketization of education systems in some countries are considered including how these might impact on system and practice developments. Positively the next part of the chapter focuses on a couple of international examples of how an inclusive whole school collaborative approach to teaching and learning can help build and maintain teacher's resilience and motivation and provide a broader resource base to help them develop the skills and knowledge to include pupils with special and other learning needs in all lessons. The chapter and thus the book conclude with a description of a future hope for a time when labels such as special educational needs are not valid or necessary in inclusive education systems around the world.

Annotated bibliography

Freeman J. (2004). 'Teaching the gifted and talented', *Education Today,* **54, pp. 17–21.** Joan Freeman has carried out much and valuable work focused on pupils who are 'gifted and talented'. In this article she discusses all of the problems and issues associated with identification and knowing how to teach these pupils. She found that just as with any other pupil those with high ability need relevant material to work with, challenging and focused tuition and encouragement, in fact a holistic approach.

She also says that 'opportunity is essential for achievement' (p. 17). Concluding, Freeman suggests that education for the most able is dependent on 'suitably trained teachers, informed parents, and most importantly the pupils themselves' (p. 17).

Schuelka, M., Thomas, G., Johnstone, C. and Artiles, A. (2019). SAGE handbook of inclusion and diversity in education. London: Sage. This is essential reading for all who want to understand more about inclusion and diversity in education. It has many contributions in chapters from across the globe considering issues from a global to a local level. It is divided into three sections: Part I is about Conceptualizations and possibilities of inclusion and diversity in education followed by Part II with a look at education practices, policies and systems. The final section Part III includes chapters about disability, diversity and inclusion from all parts of the world.

Acknowledgement

I would like to thank Christian Couper for his valued input in this chapter.

2

The Professional Self and Diverse Learning Needs

Conor Mc Guckin and Carol-Ann O'Síoráin

Introduction: Taking time

As practitioners and academics, we continually discuss with each other a general need that neither we nor our colleagues seem to attend to: taking the time to 'stop and stand and stare'. When we started our careers in education, we were full of wonderment about the work ahead, and the opportunities to become really good 'evidence-informed' educators. We were also full of optimism and enthusiasm for the pupils that we would get the opportunity to work with. We were full of hope for the transformative power of education to enhance the lives of families and communities. These are all still true. The only difference is that now we recognize how difficult it can be in an ever-evolving world.

Building on the experience and accomplishments of the Millennium Development Goals (United Nations [UN] General Assembly, 2000), the UN 'Sustainable Development Goals (SDGs)' encourage the 193 countries of the UN to make sustained efforts to transform the world through seventeen SDGs (e.g. poverty, hunger, health, well-being, education, climate change, gender equality) over the next fifteen years (UN General Assembly, 2015). The work that you do each day can make a contribution towards the realization of these global SDGs.

In this era of international accountability and change, we belong to a collective voice for education to be transformative in actions and outcomes, and to rectify previous inequalities. SDG4 (Quality Education) and SDG10 (Reduced Inequalities) require our full attention to address and promote access to an appropriate, equitable and truly inclusive experience for the children and young people in our care. This requires that we take an opportunity for honest introspection on how our attitudes, values and practices reflect an inclusive approach to gender, race, culture, language, ethnicity, disability/ability and additional needs.

As we attend to our work here in this chapter, we have been somewhat forced to 'stop and stand and stare'. As reflexive practitioners, this is an ongoing thread that many of you may identify with in the rich tapestry of being a continually developing educator. We trust that our reflections and work here will be of use to you in your own reflections and plans for the future.

It is probably fair to say that there has been a drift between our early ambitions and the reality of the contemporary classroom. This might be partly attributable to changes in policy and prevailing ideologies regarding the role of education and inclusive pedagogy. However, our own changing personal and professional identities cannot be ignored.

As we write this, we are immensely aware of the competing demands on your life and time – some from your professional life, some from your personal and family life, and some from the world that we live in. Whatever age or stage of your life you are at, we would encourage you to go on this journey with us, with an open and reflexive mind. We would encourage you to recognize all of the 'baggage' that you have accumulated on your professional and life's travels, and to de-centre from this accumulation of attitudes, perspectives, prejudices and practices. This type of work is seldom as easy as it first appears. To be truly reflective, we need to be aware of the possible need to change our mindsets and approaches to practice. If attitudinal and behavioural change was easy, we would have little need for all of the motivational and technological tools we use in our (often futile) attempts to increase the number of steps taken each day, reminders to have some 'headspace', apps to help us be more productive and lifestyle approaches to help us with the 'disease of being busy' (Safi, 2014). So, we hope the thinking tools and approaches outlined in this chapter will help you to reappraise your professional, personal, social and emotional responsibilities – to yourself and to those young hearts and minds that you are entrusted to work with.

Structuring our thinking

In your daily lives as educators, it may feel like you are being bombarded with new information, competing policy directives and conflicting research findings – all before you can begin to consider your teaching plans and methodologies, assessment for learning, assessment of learning, and meetings and reporting. And, all of this before you start to think about those pupils with a special educational need/disability, or those who are able and talented, or both (dual exceptionality).

To help you manage your workloads across these different issues, we suggest that you use a tool that we have found to be a consistent companion. This tool relates to thinking and incorporating knowledge about the relationships between Policy, Practice (provision), Experiences and Outcomes (PPEO) (also see Chapter 1). These, as well as the importance of 'communications' and 'relationships', were identified by Rose et al. (2015) in their longitudinal study that examined how special education was provided in Irish schools. We believe that PPEO, when used as an overarching structure, will help you consider your personal and professional responsibilities (personal, social and emotional) and the impact that these can have on inclusive and reflective practice – attending to the learning, social and emotional needs of pupils with whom you work.

In doing this, we are also guided by the exceptionally easy-to-understand work of Urie Bronfenbrenner (see Mc Guckin and Minton, 2014 for a useful practical example of how to use Bronfenbrenner's approach, and https://conormcguckin. com/archives/2294 for an introduction to the theory and approach). Despite the great array of educational and psychological theories that we have been exposed to, it was really the work of Bronfenbrenner that helped us to understand 'the person in context' (Bronfenbrenner, 1979, 1989). For example, whilst Piaget was useful in terms of helping us to understand cognitive development, Kohlberg in terms of moral development, and Erikson in terms of psychosocial development, none of the major theories of human development provided a framework of how we might understand all aspects of the person in the context of their ecology (environment) – i.e. their lived reality.

Bronfenbrenner's model can be used in two ways: (i) to contextualize and understand the myriad of factors directly and indirectly influencing ourselves as professionals, and (ii) to think about how this is done when working with pupils. Bronfenbrenner's nested systems model (often represented as a series of concentric two-dimensional circles – See Figure 2.1) presents a very useful and easily understood approach that can help to contextualize the information about a person that can be important.

From your own personal and professional histories, you can structure your thinking by using 'PPEO' to understand the critical influence of the various 'facilitators' and 'barriers' that exist in your own lives – be they people, policies,

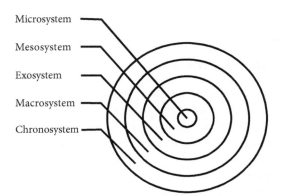

Figure 2.1 Bronfenbrenner's Ecological Model (1979, 1989) (reproduced from Mc Guckin and Minton, 2014).

practices. In Bronfenbrenner's terms – the microsystem represents the most connected ecological space to the individual, in that it generally represents the home and family environment, where interactions and supports are immediate, face-to-face and one-to-one (i.e. lots of 'E'xperiences and 'O'utcomes are visible at this level). At the next layer, the mesosystem represents the relationships that the individual and those in their microsystem have with people and organizations one-step removed from home and family life (e.g. school, neighbourhood). As with the microsystem, you would see lots of 'E'xperiences and 'O'utcomes visible at this level, as well as seeing the direct impact of both 'P'olicy and 'P'ractice'. The exosystem includes the ideological, political and economic structures that surround the individual and the components of their microsystem, such as the workplace, family social networks and community relations. In terms of PPEO, you would see lots of 'P'olicy and 'P'ractice evident here and, although events here are not directly experienced by the pupil or teacher, they can have a direct and immediate impact on 'E'xperiences and 'O'utcomes that you work to achieve. The macrosystem embodies all the broad social, political, and cultural attitudes and ideologies implicit in a society – creating a direct and potent influence on the direction of 'P'olicy. Bronfenbrenner allowed for the understanding of individual and socio-historical factors via the addition of the chronosystem (i.e. chrono = time). The chronosystem allows you to understand the potential long-term influence of personal (or cohort level) events on the individual's life (e.g. disability, significant bereavement). Using the PPEO thinking tool, you will be able to really see the impact and overlapping influences of 'P'olicy, 'P'ractice, 'E'xperiences and 'O'utcomes at this level of the person's ecosystem.

And so, in guiding a lot of your reflective work – on looking at your professional selves – it is important to think about the facilitators and barriers, the PPEO, and how you can draw a Bronfenbrenner model and add words and reflections in a structured manner. This is an easy task and allows you to 'stop and stand and stare' in relation to your personal, social and emotional responsibilities – to yourself and also to your pupils.

Reflective questions

1. Draw a Bronfenbrenner diagram. Start to complete the diagram about either yourself or a pupil that you work with. The process of doing this can be useful in stimulating thinking about what goes where!
2. Draw a stick-person at the very centre of the diagram – and consider all of the personal-level issues that you or the pupil must deal with as part of the normal experience of developing and existing as a human (e.g. illness, disability, stress, personal issues).

3. Add the inhabitants of the microsystem – e.g. mum, dad, brother(s), sister(s), pet(s), extended family, non-family – and think about the quality of each face-to-face relationship between you or the pupil and each of the individuals in this microsystem. The relationships are never the same, and the amount of influence that we have in each dyad is different.
4. Extend your Bronfenbrenner model by considering what might fit usefully in each of the other parts of the system.

Reflexive questions

1. By answering the reflective questions, have you learnt anything about your professional self, your beliefs or your values that may influence your practice to all your pupils or some of your pupils?
2. As before, think carefully and critically about what Bronfenbrenner's model might tell you about why and how you respond to pupils?

Inclusive education: Everyone's business?

In this section the evolving nature of inclusion is reviewed – from the early thinking about what inclusion might look like to the contemporary consideration that inclusion is everyone's business. Whether you are an early years educator, or work with pupils in primary or post-primary educational settings, it is no longer possible to argue that the education of pupils with a special educational need, or who are recognized as being particularly able or talented, or both is the remit of someone else.

Over the last four decades there have been consistent advances towards a more inclusive approach to the provision and education for pupils with additional needs (e.g. Warnock Report, 1978). However, you still need to reflect upon and consider the ideology and philosophy of your personal and professional approaches. The Salamanca Statement (UNESCO, 1994) progressed the notion of inclusion to focus on the removal of barriers to education and towards the participation of all pupils; thus, it could be argued, drawing attention away from difference to one of 'sameness'. An important outcome of looking to all pupils is that a focus is placed on pupils who might be particularly able or talented.

Observation of international policy and practice for inclusive provision indicates that certain themes are recurrent and dominant in the processes of inclusion. There has been a significant move away from archaic language use and a clinical (deficit) medical model of intervention towards a more person-centred and rights-based approach. Importantly, inclusion is now considered as an ongoing process and, we would argue, everyone's business – including yours. Rix (2015) however asks a pertinent question: 'Are we talking about the same thing?'

Reflective questions

1. When reviewing your school's policy on inclusion, reflect on whether it provides for a collective responsibility or individual responsibilities?
2. What are the challenges for you in relation to your professional role – perhaps in terms of personal, social and emotional responsibilities that might impact upon your ability to educate in an inclusive manner?
3. How can you use this reflection to adapt your approach to teaching? What are the things that you need to bring to conscious awareness and be aware of?

Internationally, the definition of inclusion and the definition of an effective inclusive educational environment remain wide-ranging and open to a variety of interpretations. This may initially seem frustrating and unhelpful, but what it does allow for is a flexible mindset and the possibility of deep reflexive thinking about what we do and how we 'do inclusion'. Warnock (Warnock and Brahms, 2010) posited that inclusion is about a 'sense of belonging', arguing that rarely does inclusion consider the emotional aspect of belonging, but rather that an emphasis is placed on physical positioning. Her argument requires reflection on whether pupils with additional learning requirements are considered as partners and leaders in their own decision-making and educational planning (as per Article 12 of the UN Convention: e.g. Lundy, 2007). Creating opportunities for pupils to be autonomous in the choice of placement, education planning and in their own lived experiences of education is, she posits, inclusive education.

Reflective questions

1. Inclusive education is for every pupil – not just those at the margins. How can you ensure that your approach is for *all* pupils?
2. What challenges are there to providing quality learning opportunities for everyone?

One approach that you might wish to explore is the concept of Universal Design (UD) (see www.CAST.org and www.AHEAD.ie). Originally developed as an inclusive approach to architecture, design and the built environment, the underlying principles of UD propose that any inclusive practice or environment needs to be considered from the very outset to ensure success. UD principles offer both a philosophy and a practical approach to addressing diversity and inclusion issues from the outset. UD approaches are increasingly being applied to education (e.g. UD for Learning: UDL; UD for Instruction: UDI; UD for Transition: UDT). The goal of UD is to offer any pupil an experience that affords an equality of opportunity. Whilst this may appear to be rather complicated, it is being achieved in many instances – perhaps incidentally rather than by intentional design. Can a UD approach and a tiered continuum of support help your practice? For example, Level 1 – Support for All; Level 2 – Support for Some; Level 3 – Support for a Few; and Level 4 – Support for the Individual (Quirke and McCarthy, 2020).

There is also an argument suggesting that inclusion policy is driven by economic and legislative landscapes. Well, there is some truth in this. It must be acknowledged that the political agenda to protect the government from being found neglectful is evident and that there is a required need to address equality in access and participation to education. These are macro-level issues for Bronfenbrenner. The person at the centre of the diagram might not have direct influence on issues and entities here, but these can have a very potent effect on you or the pupil.

International state funding for inclusion is significant in the budgets assigned to education. This positions education practitioners and school leaders in an accountable role. What the inclusion agenda has created is a structural and functional tension in the management of inclusive participation, policy implementation, lesson planning, teaching and learning. This is especially evident in education provision for pupils with exceptional and talented ability. Teachers and school leaders now struggle with the spectrum of learning abilities evident in the modern classroom and school. Accountability also brings a level of autonomy, and teachers and school leaders are required to justify their allocation of additional resources and to provide a profile of learning needs evidenced through continuous recording and monitoring of observations and assessments. Contemporary instructional structures such as co-teaching, team teaching and in-class additional support while evidenced as positive in general mainstream education have yet to be validated for pupils with additional learning needs. Group and/or individual teaching within the mainstream class setting is now considered best practice. Further, there is an onus on the teacher to extend and advance differentiation of lesson planning and delivery as a means of inclusive practice to facilitate a range of cognitive abilities, learning preferences and learning styles.

Professionalization of the teaching profession and the creation of standards and regulations have added to the concept of transformative education and position the

Reflective questions

1. A moment to ponder … do you think, act and plan inclusively?
2. How might you do this with more attention to the principles of UD?
3. How do you approach planning and adaptation of instruction for pupils with exceptional and talented capabilities?

professional teacher as a 'leader of learning' – thus enabling each of us, as reflexive practitioners, to make a contribution to the SDG 4 and SDG 10. The concept of a 'leader of learning' holds the premise of 'intentionality' for conscious and creative practices that can ensure quality relationships that can influence and generate change within and across educational landscapes (Woods and Roberts, 2018). A collective, collaborative and participative culture of leadership in education is encouraged at a policy level through reflective school self-evaluations to promote quality inclusive learning experiences and outcomes in our schools. Contemporary thinking about school leadership provides an interesting perspective that moves away from the traditional hierarchical approach towards a more 'distributed' approach. This approach allows for various members of the school community to assume leadership responsibilities. Salokangas and Ainscow (2018) indicate the need for all stakeholders to have a level of freedom and autonomy in decision-making for change, and to enhance curriculum, policy and provision. In particular, they draw on the role and importance of autonomous school-wide leadership for strategic and operational change.

Across Europe, the Organization for Economic Cooperation and Development (OECD, 2010) and the European Agency for the Development of Special Education (EADSNE, 2012) have influenced the structure of Initial Teacher Education (ITE). ITE providers are encouraged to improve teacher education for inclusion by merging mainstream education philosophies and methodologies with special education philosophies and methodologies. The emphasis being that effective teaching for pupils with additional education needs is effective teaching for all. ITE providers now include inclusive education in their policy documents and this is evidenced through subject modularization and research programmes. Universities and colleges through school placement modules also position reflections on inclusion as an important learning outcome for the student teacher. Placement experiences are meant to provide the student teacher with the opportunity to bring theory and practice together. While this is a welcomed direction, Robinson (2017) argues through detailed empirical research that there remains a theory and practice gap. She asserts that ITE remains too theoretically based and lacks practical realities for transferring knowledge to the classroom of the newly qualified teacher. Her research findings indicate and correlate Elliott's (1991) 'reality shock' theory, that newly qualified teachers still experience a reality shock when faced with the modern diverse classroom. Robinson's (2017) argument is important here as some pupils with a diagnosis of exceptional ability may also have an identified additional learning challenge. Such a pupil may present as being very capable in a specific subject area (mathematics, for instance) but emotionally and psychologically vulnerable. The pupil may experience self-doubt or lack the self-esteem to achieve their potential. This dual exceptionality can create a pedagogical challenge for the teacher, and being skilled at planning and adapting 'inflight thinking' (Paterson, 2007) is a practice and experience-based skill. O'Síoráin, Shevlin and Mc Guckin (2018) provide an argument for the importance of an organic nature to planning and inflight thinking for pupils with autism, where the teacher's knowledge of the pupils and the responses received during lesson implementation enable the teacher to adapt to the immediate needs of the pupils. This practice to theory approach provides an argument to – and for – an approach to differentiation that is also organic in nature. Black, Lawson and Norwich (2019, p. 122) argue that the act of teaching is an art form preceded by the scripted lesson but 'affected by interpretation and improvisation (in-flight planning)'. They contend that formal lesson planning for 'evaluative' or accountability purposes is 'far less important than the subtle and layered processes of planning before and during lessons'. Hence, the 'process of lesson planning is more important than the product' (Black, Lawson and Norwich, 2019, p. 122).

Differentiation in lesson planning is a skill developed in ITE programmes, professional learning courses and practice, but rarely does it reflect an integrated approach to pupil differences and abilities, or to differentiated pedagogical strategies. In fact, in lesson plan templates differentiation can be regularly identified as resources such as additional worksheets or adapted work sheets. Seldom does it reflect what the learning intentions are or what skills or knowledge will be achieved (Marshall, 2016). This draws attention to the need to support student teachers, early career teachers and seasoned teachers in looking at the function and purpose of formal and informal curriculum development and lesson planning.

Reflective questions

1. Review one of your lesson plans and reflect on how it supports a practice to theory approach. Does it provide you with the possibility to be flexible and responsive?
2. Have you demonstrated 'in-flight thinking'?

Professional self-care

Without asking, we are assuming that you are compassionate towards your pupils – especially those with additional difficulties. This is laudable and to be welcomed.

However, such work can be taxing on your emotional reservoir. So, make sure that you consider the key issues and hallmarks of professional self-care. As a good practitioner, you probably put a lot of attention into understanding the pupils that you work with. Do you do the same to understand yourself and your own needs? Almost akin to an IEP (Individual Education Plan), have you reflected upon your own needs and requirements?

Stress and burnout

It is well understood that teachers experience a different kind of work-related stress than other professionals. We have mentioned previously how newly qualified teachers experience a reality shock when they first begin their official qualified teaching. This reality shock is experienced when a practice to theory approach is required, and in the acknowledgement that they have embarked into the new class situation from a theory to practice (university style) approach. Across the profession, stress and burnout are common (see Chapter 3 for more information). Perhaps more common than you might first think. A similar experience can evolve in a diverse classroom, where the veteran teacher experiences a sense of discombobulation when what worked previously in resolving or addressing a need suddenly does not work. This is the case of 'one third of teachers' with a special education remit and/or when supporting pupils with emotional difficulties (Soini et al., 2019). Soini et al. (2019) assert that this evolves gradually over time and may compound a feeling of growing inadequacy and a sense of lacking in 'qualifications' to perform professionally.

Like the proverbial lobster in the pot, teachers are happy enough with surrounding heat. At the start, it is warm and cosy, heating up gradually. As it gets warmer, teachers convince themselves that the increasing heat is acceptable and that their bodies will adjust to it. However, like the lobster, it becomes too difficult to understand the difference between what is normal and what is abnormal – when stress and lack of self-care become toxic and too detrimental to health and well-being. According to Soini et al. (2019, p. 633), 'Teacher burnout is strongly context-dependent' and 'socially embedded' by the physical and cultural school environment. This surely draws attention to the professional community and the need to provide a collaborative response to supporting pupils with dual exceptionality and many other pupils learning needs?

Reflexive questions

1. What keeps you motivated and engaged in the profession of teaching?
2. What challenges this motivation and how do you protect yourself? Try journaling your thoughts and experiences and then reflect on how your behaviours could be attributed to positive and/or negative experiences.

Case study: Mainstream primary school classroom for pupils with diverse learning needs: Let's talk about John

Country: Ireland

Age group: 8–12 years

Setting: Special education primary classroom

Participants involved:

Pupil, family, teacher, Educational Welfare Officer, Family Support Workers

The case study

When John was enrolled by his parents into my special education primary classroom for young children with 'social and emotional challenges', there was no mention of his ability. His behaviours, both in his home and in the community, had brought him to the attention of medical and psychological professionals. His family had been identified as of low social and economic ability and status, and long-term educational disadvantage had impacted on the family and their ability to support John. John had not experienced success in previous school placements and the Educational Welfare Officer began liaising with the parents to ensure that John would attend school regularly. Family support workers were assigned to the family to support and help the family create a routine of attending to the educational needs, health and well-being of John. John was collected by a family worker every day and brought to school. At age eight John could not read, write, or attend to any of his peer-age academic tasks, and educational psychological assessments were incomplete because of family issues that occurred during planned testing. As a teacher receiving John into the classroom, I had no previous information to refer to, and no medical or psychological information – John was just John.

Teacher: Self-reflections

What is important about this situation is that without the possible imposing tensions of 'medical' or 'ecological' perspectives to inclusive education approaches, I had free reign to get to know John himself. Now, this could be daunting for a teacher, and I will be honest when I say I wondered 'where is the starting point?', and 'how do I know I'm doing things right or doing the right things?' When the educational psychologist came to conference with me to explore 'professionally' how we would provide for John, he asked me what ideas I had about lessons and tasks. I replied that I needed to understand firstly how John plays, how he communicates, how he manages relationships with his peers, and what his likes and dislikes are. This personal and professional philosophy of the relational context for teaching and learning was an essential starting point to a very successful outcome for both John and his family.

Outcome: Partnership in leading learning

It was not plain sailing! John's physical behaviours were challenging and while he was slight in stature he was a force to be reckoned with among his equally challenging peers. John joined a class of seven other boys his own age, all with a dual diagnosis of mild/moderate general learning disability and either a physical, emotional, sensory, neurodevelopmental disability, and/or ADHD. What was different about John was that he had exceptional ability and was diagnosed two years later with Asperger syndrome. Myself (as teacher) along with two supporting special needs assistants (SNA) established a practical partnership and routine of practice. We realized immediately that John had little experience of observing adults working and communicating in harmony. John's parents had experienced high levels of stress relating to marital and family life issues. Modelling relationships, reciprocity and self-regulation became the educational prime focus. As a teaching team, we modelled reading and writing, we practised problem-solving and problem-posing scenarios, we dramatized life issues, and we took on numeracy from a literacy perspective using basic life mathematics to draw attention to the fact that we live in a mathematical world. We gave basic IT skills and enabled John to explore his own interests (with certain restrictions). John became self-motivated and directed us to listen to his new ideas and learning experiences. John gave us confidence to hand over certain aspects of the decision-making and curriculum planning to our other pupils too.

Window on research

The role of home-school support

This window into research allows you to see the clear and important link between the home environment of a pupil and their school experiences. In terms of Bronfenbrenner, this demonstrates the important interface between the microsystem (i.e. home) and the mesosystem (e.g. relationship between home and school).

We know from Erik Erikson's (1950) psychosocial theory that the social and emotional development of all children begins at birth and takes root in the face-to-face relationships with those in the microsystem (i.e. immediate family/caregivers). To establish important lifelong psychological characteristics (e.g. a sense of trust, autonomy, self-belief, motivation, personal identity, belonging, love), children depend upon strong, stable, and consistent care and nurturing. Such stability enables young children to navigate their increasing social circles and provides feedback on established social norms – important for relationships at the mesosystem level – e.g. school, sports clubs, local neighbourhood friendships. Family structure and positive functioning are, therefore, essential elements to the development of self-regulation in the social and emotional behaviour of children as they transition and engage in education across their lifespan.

A diagnostic characteristic of autism relates to the social interaction and communication domain. Children and young people with autism often struggle with social realities and experience high levels of anxiety that may result in what appears to typically developing persons as 'anti-social' behaviours (Fletcher-Watson and Happé, 2019). Parents of children who have autism can experience high levels of stress that can contribute to challenges within their own relationships, and this can have an impact on the function and role of the family in its caregiving duties (O'Síoráin, 2017).

In O'Síoráin's (2017) research, parents of children with autism described themselves as 'other' – not belonging any more to their own social groups – and feeling distanced from their extended families. Preece and Howley (2018) note that the role of quality experiences in school is evidenced as 'good practice' in autism education. They provide a substantial argument that pupils with autism who experience high levels of anxiety can become school refusers as they progress through the system, creating a further stress within families. They argue that quality home-school relationships (i.e. the relationship between the micro and mesosystem) are essential in reducing the anxiety experienced by the pupil with autism and the stress experienced by the parents/caregivers. Supporting the ecological perspective, Preece and Howley provide evidence that the wider community of the school can lead to better learning outcomes – if there is a focus on the uniqueness and identified needs of the individual, whilst also acknowledging parental/family concerns.

Reflective questions

1. From the case example above and building on your knowledge of the Bioecological systems model (Bronfenbrenner), consider the relational aspects of leadership and management you use when supporting pupils with exceptional ability and/or additional needs.
2. What relational leadership skills do you require to work in a team and to lead a team within the classroom?
3. At what point in your lesson planning and curriculum development do you allow the pupils to lead learning? In your next lesson planning can you identify how the voice and preferences of the pupil can support you in an authentic pathway to inclusive teaching and learning?

Case study: Disablist bullying

Country: Northern Ireland and the Republic of Ireland

Setting: Initial teacher education

Participants involved: Trainee teachers

As already noted, teachers are often very good at using their knowledge gained in ITE and professional learning to develop good learning opportunities for pupils with learning, social and emotional needs. This often necessitates thinking critically about how to 'mix' the knowledge gained regarding specific issues (e.g. ADHD, dyslexia) and methodologies (e.g. differentiation for assessment for learning). However, curriculum issues are not the only challenges confronting many of these pupils.

Purdy and Mc Guckin (2014) were interested in the knowledge, experience and confidence of student teachers in relation to what they termed disablist bullying. That is, how good were they at 'mixing' knowledge of additional learning requirements and bullying behaviour – a non-curricular issue that can disproportionately affect the pupils with additional needs (e.g. United States: Carter and Spencer, 2006; England: Norwich and Kelly, 2004). The research argued that (i) due to the central importance of the issue in teacher training, student teachers should be able to demonstrate good levels of knowledge and confidence regarding the additional requirements of their pupils, (ii) they should have gained some knowledge of bully/victim problems through their education (e.g. perhaps only one lecture), but (iii) they would struggle with demonstrating knowledge and confidence of dealing with both of these issues when they arose at the same time (i.e. in a case of bully/victim problems involving a pupil with an additional learning requirement – 'disablist' bullying).

Not one of the student teachers in the research had received any course content whatsoever during their ITE in relation to disablist bullying. Despite this universal lack of preparation, 8 per cent ($n = 19$) had dealt with one incident, 4 per cent ($n = 9$) had dealt with two incidents, and 1 per cent ($n = 2$) had dealt with three incidents of disablist bullying during their teaching practice placements.

A useful example from the research was in relation to when the perpetrator of the bullying behaviour was a pupil with an additional learning requirement. One of the student teachers recounted an experience in relation to one 11 year-old boy with spina bifida who was 'very snide with people' and who 'was able … to really, really get at people'. The student teacher confessed that he found this extremely difficult to deal with:

> I would take the most classes for P.E. and [he] would play up you know
> if we were playing football ah [he] would just, ah, kick somebody's
> leg, just trip them because they were running past him and somebody
> would fall, ah, how do I, how do I deal with that? To the other ones I'd

> give them a wee fundamental movement skills exercise to do, can't give it to [him], he's physically disabled. I found it very, very difficult to find any way of sort of reprimanding him, so yes, by necessity the bullying was almost tolerated.

What we can learn

This student teacher has identified that school environments are not always safe (Smit and Scherman, 2016). When issues of bullying like this occur, Smit and Scherman (2016) argue that the relational aspects of trust and respect are challenged. They contend that the social structures of the school as a community are based on 'acceptable social and moral behaviours' and 'school leaders play a critical role in the socialisation of learners of what constitutes acceptable behaviour' (Smit and Scherman, 2016, p. 1). In this instance, the student teacher as a leader of learning could not adapt their established strategy of behaviour management and class recovery. It could be argued that a simple direct verbal instruction to cease such inappropriate behaviour is warranted – however, Smit and Scherman (2016) suggest that bullying requires a relational and interactional approach to successfully lead learning and maintain social structures in the classroom and school.

For a different student teacher, there was even less certainty about how to respond, explaining that through his ITE education they had never touched on the causes or impact of bullying, and admitted that his reaction to a bullying incident would be to deal with it purely instinctively:

> You deal with it naturally. And that has the potential to be an ineffective reaction. I mean I don't know, or, I don't know why or what causes bullying; I don't know what the outcomes for people that are bullied are. I mean formally I've never, I've never even touched on it.

When asked what would guide their response to such issues, just over one-third (35 per cent, $n = 90$) reported similarly, in that they would rely on 'natural instinct'.

As with many issues that confront you in the classroom, there simply is not time or space in the ITE curriculum to explore every possible scenario. Indeed, even with copious amounts of professional learning, there will still be novel issues that will need creative and confident thinking and collaboration.

Noted in this case example was the under-preparedness of the student teachers, who relied on ad hoc and ill-conceived approaches. Notable also is the lack of a leadership identity, where leading the learning is more about 'care, vision, collaboration, courage, intuition and dialogue' (Smit and Scherman, 2016, p. 3).

Reflective questions

1. Consider the research on relational leadership. Have you established a leadership identity? Was a 'natural instinct' approach sufficient?
2. What would have been a useful approach to the issues in the case example? As well as using our PPEO thinking tool, you might also seek answers to questions that are framed as: Who?, What?, When?, Where?, Why? and Which?

Outcome

Issues like this can serve to re-traumatize a teacher if the teacher has previously unresolved issues (e.g. dealing with pupil-related bereavement and grief issues whilst still working through personal issues related to a bereavement: Lynam, McConnell and Mc Guckin, 2018; O'Brien and Mc Guckin, 2014).

Of course a compassionate approach to such issues is recommended – for the pupil and, importantly, for you. However, 'honesty without compassion is cruelty'.

So, in terms of thinking about this case example, and the myriad of other case examples that you could draw upon that present real challenges to your work with pupils, how do you as a professional recognize your own personal, social and emotional responsibilities?

Reflexive question

Do you challenge and question your own assumptions about the issue? We all have our own internal prejudices. This is normal. However, when these are not challenged, actions based on prejudicial thoughts become discriminatory actions.

Implications for educators

At the start of this chapter it was acknowledged that teachers will all be leading busy personal and professional lives. For some colleagues, this has unfortunately resulted in job-related stress and burnout. With this in mind, we invited you to do something that many of us do not feel that we have the time to do – to 'stop and stand and stare'. As professionals, it is important to participate in continual professional development and to be reflexive practitioners. But, amidst the bustle of modern life, challenging your own attitudes and changing your behaviours are not always easy to do.

Recognizing the implications of not being reflexive practitioners, useful 'thinking tools' were introduced. As educators, you are always rooted in ensuring that pupils and families have good 'E'xperiences, and 'O'utcomes, but you also need to think about your 'P'ractice and how this is influenced by 'P'olicy.

It was also recognized that everyone's lived reality is different – perhaps more so for those pupils who have a special educational need, or are exceptionally talented and able, or both. In thinking about the multiple influences on a person's life (both facilitators and barriers), and how these can have an important influence on their ability to function at the most optimal level, Bronfenbrenner's ecological framework was explored to help you understand these influences.

The key task of remembering that inclusion of all pupils is everyone's business was discussed through reflecting on relevant research studies, alongside attending to your own your personal, social and emotional needs.

As we bid farewell for now, we would encourage you to keep reflecting on your practice and responsibilities, and the wider issues that we have raised in this chapter. Moving forwards, what do you personally, socially and emotionally need to consider?

Annotated bibliography

Bronfenbrenner, U. (1979). *The ecology of human development: Experiments by nature and design.* **Cambridge, MA: Harvard University Press.**
This is the classic book by Bronfenbrenner. It has really changed how psychologists and many other professionals see the life of children and young people. The model that Bronfenbrenner presents is immediately understandable and practically useful. It is also very beneficial in that there is no right or wrong way in which to use the model. We would really encourage you to explore how this approach can help you 'de-clutter' your mind and paperwork – presenting a ready-made structure in which we can catalogue all of the important information about the pupil at the centre of their ecology.

Lundy, L. (2007). '"Voice" is not enough: Conceptualising Article 12 of the United Nations Convention on the Rights of the Child', *British Educational Research Journal,* **33(6), pp. 927–42. doi:10.1080/01411920701657033**
As an educator with a fine legal mind, Laura Lundy has done much to emphasize that 'pupil voice' is central to the work that we do. If we are to achieve a society where everyone can access education and make real choices regarding independent living and being equal citizens, then it is useful to recognize 'pupil voice' and how it can help us deliver education that is equitable in an ever-developing diverse society.

Quirke, M. and McCarthy, P. (2020). *A conceptual framework of Universal Design for Learning (UDL) for the Irish Further Education and Training Sector: 'Where Inclusion is Everyone's Business'*. Dublin, Ireland: SOLAS.

The Universal Design for Learning (UDL) (social model) approach is something that every teacher should be aware of. UDL really acknowledges the importance of active inclusion. This publication is an easy-to-access introduction to the theory and practice of UDL.

Safi, O. (2014, November 6). *The disease of being busy.* [Blog post]. Available at: https://onbeing.org/blog/the-disease-of-being-busy/

This is an easy-to-access and easy-to-read article that pointedly highlights the modern discourse of the need to be able to report to friends that we are 'mad busy'. It is a useful read in that it helps you to 'stop and stand and stare' – and reflect upon whether we are working in a safe and healthy manner.

3
Health and Well-Being
Alan Bainbridge and Alison Ekins

Reflecting on the impact of health and well-being for everyone within the school setting is crucial, having two different, but equally important, elements to it. It not only refers to the importance of recognizing and supporting the personal health and well-being of the pupils that you work with, but also refers to the importance of acknowledging and addressing the significant impact that supporting pupils' complex needs and the impact of significant changes within the education system have on teachers themselves. Neither sits in isolation, but rather there is a complex and interconnected relationship between the well-being of staff and pupils, with each impacting the other. Writing about such a relationship often requires a level of artificial separation that does not represent real life. We try to represent this intimate relationship within our writing and boundaries between teacher and pupil, indeed teacher and spouse can, rightly, become blurred.

This chapter therefore provides an overview of the increasingly complex health, well-being and medical needs of pupils that as teachers you will increasingly come face-to-face with. It also explores the health, well-being and resilience of those education professionals who have leadership responsibilities around SEN, health needs and inclusion for creating an environment where the pupils in their charge are cared for. Our focus will be on the importance of caring for the carer, acknowledging that unless individuals can value and look after themselves, it will be less likely that the professional judgements necessary to provide effective care to young people in education settings will be made. We provide some case study examples of approaches that can be taken to support with this, and some recommendations for ways that professionals, both those established within the profession, and those that are new to the profession, can find strategies and support to mitigate against issues such as fatigue, stress and lack of confidence. We offer a definition of stress that includes internal or external factors that are likely to cause individuals persistent psychological and physical discomfort. Particularly, in the context of 'burn-out' where staff may have encountered continual demands that finally lead to the inability to carry out their professional role. These will of course be contextual and present very differently. (The details will be explored in the case studies.)

To begin, we offer a brief overview of the challenging context for professionals working in schools, as a background to our discussions about the importance of creating school systems which actively recognize, acknowledge and address the health and well-being of all its school community – to include both pupils and their families, and the professionals that work within the school. Additionally, acknowledging that comparatively recent developments in education settings have made the roles, particularly those associated with SEN, challenging.

Through this chapter, we encourage you to reflect on the following broad questions:

As a teacher what do you personally, socially and emotionally need to consider in relation to each of the following elements:

- Personal responsibility?
- Emotional responsibility to self?
- Social responsibility to others including pupils, colleagues, family and members of the local community?
- Are there any other areas of responsibility that you need to be aware of and consider?

Context

A challenging school context in England

For over thirty years, schools have been under pressure to 'perform' to high standards and achieve 'outstanding' exam results, occupying lofty positions in local and national league tables, to prepare for inspections by the English Inspection body Ofsted, while attempting to balance a precarious budget and this has placed, and continues to place, schools under considerable stress.

With the increase in financial and accountability pressures in schools and education as a whole, and the recent rapid changes in systems underpinning work in schools in England (including the new SEN and Disability code of practice, 2014/2015; the new OFSTED School Inspection Framework, 2019), school professionals are finding themselves under increased and sustained pressure to be able to meet the needs of the pupils and communities that they serve.

The consequences of these political decisions are complex and have led to significant strains being placed on all teachers to not only deliver an academic curriculum but alongside this, with the support of increasingly over-stretched SENCOs, care for the social, emotional and general health of their pupils.

It is now well-accepted, at least in England, that since the introduction of the new legislative approach to SEND in 2014, with the updated SEN and Disability code of practice (DfE and DoH, 2014), embedded education systems, not only in individual schools, but significantly nationally and in Local Authorities, have not been able to cope with the requirements of the new approach (HoC, 2019). As the National Audit Office (2019) notes, 'In 50% of inspections [of Local Authorities] OFSTED and the CQC [Care Quality Commission] found areas of weakness significant enough to require the local areas to prepare a written statement of action in response' (NAO, 2019, p. 46).

This has, as a result, had a significant impact on staff working with pupils who have the most vulnerable and complex needs in their schools. Not only are the staff within the school setting overloaded with the level of complex needs that they are working with, but currently, in many areas, they do not have the support of carefully structured processes and systems to manage the increased responsibilities of the new SEN and Disability Code of Practice (DfE/DoH, 2014/ 2015) at a Local Authority level. This, in many areas, has increased the tensions between parents and the Local Authority, and subsequently caused increased workload (including increased requests for statutory assessment documentation, evidence for Local Authority SEN and Disability Tribunals etc.) and stress for SENCOs and other professionals working in schools as they try to mediate and provide effective support.

The resulting increased workload, although distributed throughout all staff, particularly falls within the remit of SENCOs and the wider SEN and also pastoral care teams, involving working alongside children, families (and communities) to resolve issues related to domestic violence, sexual abuse, drug and alcohol addiction, gang violence, children as carers and homelessness.

Consequently, teachers in England and other parts of the UK and indeed across other parts of the world are now required to not only meet the expected national professional Teacher Standards, but also manage the complex social, emotional and often medical needs of the pupils in their care. Recent research (Jerrim et al., 2020) highlights that one in twenty teachers report mental health problems lasting for at least twelve months alongside an increase in prescribed antidepressant medication. We argue that the accumulation of these complex professional, personal and often disturbing demands is having a negative impact on attracting colleagues into the profession and then once in make retention less likely. Additionally, research now consistently shows the proportion of teachers staying in the profession after one, two and three years is steadily decreasing alongside an increasing number of teachers who leave within their first year (Worth et al., 2018).

It is also significant that the new OFSTED inspection framework (2019) recognizes the above dilemma highlighting the need for the well-being of staff to be included in the leadership and management aspect of the inspection process. The message offered by this inclusion is that effective organizations must be led by people who are aware of and responsive to the impact of working in school settings on the emotional lives of their staff. In order to achieve an 'outstanding' in leadership and management, settings must be able to demonstrate a meaningful engagement with, and consistently quick responses to, staff well-being issues.

Reflective questions

1. What challenges do you experience, or are already aware of, in your own setting and work?
2. Are the challenges that you experience increasing, or decreasing?
3. Why is this – what are the factors that are challenging?
4. What support do you already receive to help you to manage those challenges?
5. What additional support do you think would be effective in helping you to be able to respond positively to challenges that you experience teaching children with complex needs?

Reflexive question

Do you feel any of your own emotional/mental health needs are being supported or considered?

Understanding health and medical needs

There are increasing numbers of pupils with a range of health and medical conditions, including those with life-limiting conditions, who now attend mainstream schools and are the responsibility of the educational professionals within the school setting (DfE, 2015; Ekins et al., 2017). Whilst school staff are well used to their responsibilities in relation to common health and medical conditions (asthma, hay fever etc.), as a result of technological and medical advancements, schools are now seeing increasing numbers of pupils with more complex and indeed life-limiting or life-threatening conditions. In response to this, schools are recognizing that they need to develop systems and processes for ensuring that statutory responsibilities for the education and healthcare of the pupils whilst they are in school is not only in place, but effective (Ekins et al., 2017).

Life-limiting conditions include 'those from which there is no reasonable hope of cure and from which children or young people will die' (Ekins et al., 2017, p. 3). Life-threatening conditions are 'those for which curative treatment may be possible but can fail'. These include:

- Conditions in which medical treatment may fail (e.g. cancer, organ failure and HIV/AIDS)

- Conditions in which the pupil has long periods of intensive treatment and in which premature death is possible (e.g. cystic fibrosis, Duchenne muscular dystrophy)
- Progressive conditions for which there is no cure (e.g. Batten's disease, muscular dystrophy, cerebral palsy, mucopolysaccharidoses)
- Conditions in which pupils have a severe neurological disability which could lead to death (e.g. complex needs such as those following brain or spine injuries, severe cerebral palsy) (based on Association for Children's Palliative Care, 2009) (Ekins et al., 2017, p. 3).

Even though there is recognition through recent national policy development (DfE, 2015) of the need for schools to recognize and positively address the medical and health needs of pupils in their care, research continues to highlight the continued lack of coherent support and systems to ensure that educational professionals are being given the information and skills that they need (Ekins et al., 2017). Consequently, school leaders and individual teachers now feel unsure about how to meet the needs of pupils with health and medical needs (Robinson and Summers, 2012), and this continues to be the case, adding to the stress that they feel about the extended expectations and responsibilities that have been added to their roles, and which sit outside of their educational expertise.

In addition to the increase in pupils with identified health and medical needs, schools have also seen an increase in the numbers of those with identified mental health, social and emotional needs.

Case study: Educating pupils with life-limiting conditions

Country: UK

Dates: 2014–present day

Age group: Primary and Secondary teachers working with 4–18-year-olds

Subject: Understanding the emotional impact of working with pupils with complex medical conditions

What happened

The Teaching for Life research project (Ekins et al., 2017) looked at the needs of teachers working in mainstream school settings in relation to ways that they can be supported to understand and meet the needs of pupils with a range of core complex medical conditions.

The findings identified real willingness and a commitment to support the pupil and their family as much as possible through a range of very individualized approaches, but also identified high levels of anxiety by teachers about whether they were fully equipped and skilled to be able to do the 'right thing' for pupils with complex medical conditions. This included feelings such as those represented below: 'I'm scared of getting something wrong or making a situation worse or not dealing with something in the correct way.' (Teacher)

'We're frightened quite often to do certain things because we've got that fear of doing it wrong, not doing it correctly, at the wrong time.' (Teacher)

'I'd be concerned about how I would talk about this to the student and their family.' (Teacher)

'I don't think that we are prepared for it [the death of a child with a life limiting illness], I think that it's going to be quite devastating to the staff and probably the children, because it is going to hit them in such a big way in school.' (Teacher)

'If he was to pass away under our care he would have been a classmate of 28 other 8-year old children. How are we going to manage that positively and enable children to grieve? If a child in the class were to die, how do you .... I don't think I'd even know where to start with that.' (Teacher)

'When the first child died there was absolutely no support, I was busking it and I felt very vulnerable. The teachers were very upset, the parents were very upset, obviously devastated. The other children were very upset and I was making it up as I went along.' (Teacher)

Outcomes

As a result of the research that was completed, awareness was raised of the need to provide mainstream school teachers with much more information and frameworks for support to help them to understand and manage the needs of pupils with complex medical and health conditions (Ekins et al., 2017).

Reflective questions

1. If you have had experience of working with and meeting the needs of pupils with complex medical conditions and life-limiting illnesses, how did this impact on you personally, professionally, emotionally?
2. What additional support do you think would have been helpful? How could you access this?

Social, emotional and mental health needs

In England and other UK nations, the social, emotional and mental health (SEMH) needs of pupils are being acknowledged and included within national policy and systems (DfE and DoH, 2014, 2015). This has enabled a shift in thinking in education, recognizing that behavioural needs are the symptom and expression of underlying difficulties, and do not accurately reflect the key underlying need itself. This shift has therefore encouraged a different approach to understanding and responding to behavioural needs, helping teachers working in schools to think more deeply about whether the presenting behaviour is a symptom or expression of underlying learning, communication or mental health needs and difficulties.

As a result of this, and a wider societal recognition of mental health needs, teachers are now seeing and responding to a growing range of increasingly complex mental health needs within their school context. In terms of the identification of SEN, SEMH is now the third most prevalent area of need in England, after moderate learning difficulties and speech, language and communication needs (NAO, 2019). This, however, will not represent the full picture of mental health needs that are experienced in your schools. There will also be increasing numbers of pupils who have not been identified as having SEN who experience sudden mental health difficulties, particularly as they progress through adolescence and their teenage years. One such group is the pupils who are able or talented. Whilst these may not initially be as noticeable as the needs of pupils with a special educational need, pupils who are more able can also experience significant emotional and social pressures. Teachers therefore also need to be able to identify and monitor closely any additional or increasing levels of stress that could build into mental health needs for pupils who are more able. It is important to remember that pupils who are more able may therefore experience stress and anxiety trying to sustain or 'live up' to academic expectations, and these academic expectations may be self-imposed, imposed by parents, or by teachers within the school setting themselves. Ways to acknowledge those stresses and find positive and proactive ways to address them therefore need to be planned within the school setting.

The UK is not the only country experiencing these difficulties and indeed children and young people's mental health needs is a global concern with numbers rising year on year. For example, in Australia, Hall et al. (2019, p. 5) report that 'almost one quarter (24.2%) of 15- to 19-year-olds met the criteria for psychological distress' and 'adolescents struggling the most reported they were five times less likely to seek help than those without psychological distress (36.5% compared with 7.0%)'. Nordic countries, such as Finland (Välimaa et al., 2007), and the United States (Anderson and Cardoza, 2016) also indicate increases in numbers of children and young people with mental health issues.

Unfortunately, insufficient specialist service provider (e.g. the Children's and Young People Mental Health Services (ChYPMHS) in England) capacity to meet these growing demands means there are increasing challenges for teachers who work with pupils with mental health needs on a daily basis. Teachers are not trained mental health workers yet are paradoxically the ones that are at the forefront of needing to provide vital and direct support to pupils with increasingly complex mental health needs and their families. This raises levels of stress as many teachers feel concerned about their ability to provide effective support to meet the needs of the pupils they are working with.

Increasingly, the significant impact of this on teachers and other staff members is being recognized and acknowledged, and the notion of 'secondary traumatic stress' has been introduced to recognize the impact on teachers of supporting pupils who have had a traumatic experience. If this is not enough, such stress can then be compounded further when the teacher or support person has their own personal experiences of mental health difficulties, as the needs and difficulties that the child presents with and tries to share within the school setting. This can, at times, trigger memories of personal experiences for the education professional not trained to effectively manage such situations and conversations.

It is therefore essential that every teacher as well as school leaders recognize the impact that the increasingly complex needs of the pupils they are working with may have on their personal lives.

Case study: Recognizing the emotional impact on teachers

Country: UK

Dates: 2008–present

Participants: Primary teachers working with 4–11-year-olds

Subject: The emotional impact of teaching on teacher well-being

What happened

As part of qualitative Doctoral research (Ekins, 2017) to explore the development of inclusive practices in schools, data was captured in the form of learning conversations with teachers to try to identify the key, consistent or individualized elements that support or inhibit the development of inclusive practices.

What had not been expected through this research was the really strong emotional element that was presented by teachers – their own sense of moral responsibility, and the impact that supporting pupils with a range of social, emotional and mental health needs has on their own well-being.

This then became one of the central findings from this research, emphasizing the need to recognize the strong emotional attachment and impact that teaching has on staff within the school context. In the examples from the data below, you can really hear the emotional impact on teachers, at all ages and stages in their teaching career, of working to meet the needs of pupils with a range of social, emotional and mental health needs:

'We are not just their teachers, we are their aunts and their uncles, and this is exactly how I view these children.' (Teacher)

'I just sit there going there's more to life than this, you know, you don't have to teach in a school like this … I think I'm going to give it one more year. I think for my own sanity maybe I need to get out.' (Teacher)

'At first I dreaded coming into school … The first term was horrendous, just in terms of getting to grips with all the different children, all the different needs, and working out how best to tackle each child.' (Teacher)

'It got to the point where I was really unable to cope.' (Teacher)

'It's unmanageable.' (Teacher)

'I came here and hated it with a passion. It was such a shock. You go home so tired.' (Teacher)

'I lost the will to live' (Teacher)

'It was like a living nightmare.' (Teacher)

'I haven't run out of the door. I sometimes cry myself to sleep, but I haven't run out of the door.' (Teacher)

It is the intense force of the emotional and desperate voices above that need to be understood within the context of education in our schools today, and the incredible impact that the day-to-day struggle to manage increasingly complex needs has on our teachers in terms of their own well-being and potential burnout.

Yet, through the research, often within the same learning conversations, despite the desperation and the intense emotional impact that the teachers clearly experienced, they also voiced the positive rewards of working tirelessly to deliver inclusive education and opportunities to the children that they worked with, and this shows the determination and underlying sense of moral purpose embedded in so many teachers:

'It has been horrendous, but it's been a huge learning curve. I wouldn't change it for the world.' (Teacher)

'It's so rewarding!' (Teacher)

'The stories of these children just gets under your skin' (Head teacher)

'It's extraordinary, it's phenomenal, it's certainly fantastic, it inspires me.' (Teacher)

'The rewards are amazing!' (Teacher)

Outcomes

The strong positive, and negative, emotional feelings that were expressed by teachers in relation to how they were meeting the challenging social, emotional and mental health needs of the pupils and families that they were working with were highlighted as an unexpected and unanticipated key finding of the research.

Reflexive questions

1. Do any of the quotations presented in the case study above resonate with how you have felt at times when working with pupils with mental health needs?
2. How has it made you feel and how do you cope with it?

Reflective questions

1. Consider a time when you have been anxious about an issue or worried about someone or something; how do you think it impacted on your ability to work with pupils with social, emotional and mental health needs?
2. Where do you go for support and how do you think it impacts on your own personal resilience?

Support and supervision in education settings

As the discussions in this chapter so far have identified, there is now a real need for education professionals, and particularly school leaders, to consider the impact of complex health and mental health needs on everyone in the school community – including teachers.

This next section of the chapter therefore explores what school leaders and education leaders can do to help themselves and teachers cope with and maintain and even develop their professional resilience when working with pupils with mental health and/or special educational needs. It will also look at a couple of practical recommendations which could be useful and appropriate in your school.

Interventions including coaching, mentoring and supervision have begun to emerge as potential solutions, not only for recruitment and retention but also as a means to provide care for those who are working in complex and demanding educational situations. For example, this now includes the recent establishment of The National Hub for Supervision in Education by the Carnegie School of Education at Leeds Beckett University (Internet 1). Their intention is to provide dedicated supervisors to work with schools and provide in-school training for teachers, including head teachers, SENCOs and safeguarding leads to enable them to set up supervision for staff in their own schools, whilst also providing them with support from an experienced external supervisor.

Window on research

Other pieces of research and supervision delivery programmes are also being carried out around the country including at Canterbury Christ Church University. An initial small-scale research study exploring the impact of a community supervision service for colleagues in schools (Reid and Soan, 2015, 2018) led to the development of a model of supervision and support now currently being researched (Bainbridge, Reid and Del Negro, 2019), drawing attention to enabling the supervisee to identify and explore a particular aspect of professional practice, and importantly identify their own plan for the future. The most recent findings, based on the analysis of a series of rich contextual narratives, highlight the overwhelming positive impact of clinical supervision and support providing three general positive outcomes: professional learning; health and well-being; effect on school. The findings below offer some insight into how this process of supervision can have a positive impact on a school leader, Clare.

During the period of supervision, Clare was able to step out of the role of a 'do-er' into a more thoughtful position, particularly one that had time to consider what her colleagues might be thinking of her actions. The two-hour supervision sessions briefly distanced Clare from the busy-ness of school life; taking time away from the normal duties, Clare was able to move from 'do-er' to thinker. The space for supervision provided an opportunity for Clare to be able to speak out without fear of being judged, or for her to feel that her staff would question her position and ability. The opportunity for Clare to 'dig deeper' during supervision reduced her levels of stress and anxiety, claiming that she slept better and acknowledged wider benefits:

> I would say the benefit in my private life has been really – because I am able to talk about things and then leave them at school, whereas before I was coming home and saying to my partner 'what do you think about this – I've done this?

Clare regarded the impact of supervision to 'be huge' both at school and at home; she offers a simple but effective way forward for her professional learning:

> I think I know what I need to do, 'can you just let me sit and talk around what I need to do, then go off and do it'. Rather than spend the next three hours of my evening worrying that I've done it right. So yeah the impact on me was huge.

The process of supervision has enabled Clare to reflect on practice and make decisions that she is comfortable with; importantly, it has also met what can be regarded as the moral obligation to care for school leaders, and, in doing so, those in their care.

Outcome:

The process of supervision enabled Clare to reflect on practice and make decisions that she is comfortable with and she feels in control of. As a head teacher and teacher, she is able to explore her thoughts, reflect and also be reflexive in a safe, calm environment.

Reflective questions

1. Are you given the opportunity to have supervision when needed?
2. If not, reflect on how you feel it would help you personally, socially and emotionally?

> ## Reflexive question
>
> Do you think supervision might provide you with the space and opportunity to consider your own feelings and perhaps beliefs which might impact on your professional practice when working with pupils with additional needs?

What we can learn

If your school is considering providing supervision for teachers and other staff members, it is important to remember that they should be set up under the direction of an experienced supervisor. This could be someone from a health profession who is already experienced in supportive clinical supervision practices and can be linked very specifically to the medical or mental health needs of an individual or small number of pupils with identified needs, or could be someone with experience of educational supervision. This must always be set up in an appropriate way; so advice, support and guidance to understand the notion and practice of supervision and to set it up in effective ways must be sought prior to implementation.

Other ways you and your school can focus on meeting health and well-being needs

Individual healthcare plans and/or risk assessments

These should be detailed, individual plans to clearly set out and explain the healthcare or mental healthcare needs of an individual pupil, and the steps that need to be taken by the school to meet those needs. These are really important documents, which should be set up in close liaison and discussion with the pupil's parents, relevant healthcare professionals and, when possible and appropriate, the pupil themselves. They will also provide you – the teacher – with the confidence and reassurance that you are doing what is medically/psychologically most appropriate for the pupil.

Clear procedures and policies for grief, loss and bereavement

Bereavement in a school community can happen at any time, as a result of a sudden tragic accident. It can also be something that is expected to happen at some point, in the example of a pupil with a known life-limiting or life-threatening condition. It can be helpful to the school community and particularly to the teacher if plans are clearly set out for when/if a pupil from the school dies in advance so everything can be objectively considered, discussed and revised ahead of the situation occurring when emotions will be running high.

Healthcare information sheets and fact

Files about key medical and mental health needs: Establishing positive and collaborative working practices with key health professionals will be essential to ensuring that you, the teacher, have the knowledge, understanding and support to be able to meet the needs of pupils causing concern or with complex needs in the school setting. Work towards identifying a 'directory' of key contacts so that, should new symptoms or needs arise, you know who to contact for advice and support. Where possible, ask health professionals to provide information sheets, fact-files and training about both the general medical condition or mental health need, and also the specific details in relation to how the individual pupil presents. Your SENCO (in England) or Specialist SEN teacher will also be able to provide you with advice and support with this.

Review of curriculum

An understanding and support of well-being for you or the pupils should not be seen as an 'add-on'. It should be something that should be fully embedded in the school and across the curriculum. As a class teacher, subject tutor or school leader, you should therefore also consider carefully ways that the general and specific needs of pupils with additional needs within the school community can be reflected within the curriculum that is developed and delivered, and ways that well-being can be addressed and reflected throughout.

Positive role-modelling

Here all school community members should consider carefully ways that as a whole it can model a healthy lifestyle across the life and activities of the school. This should include consideration of:

1. The *food choices* that are available, both at lunchtime and throughout the day in the food that is allowed/encouraged at break times and before and after school. It can also include specific planning for teaching about cooking, shopping and making healthy food choices. Don't forget to also think about this when you are 'rewarding' children. This can be a particular issue when working with pupils with a special educational need or who are engaged in individual research (high ability).
2. The *healthy physical activities* that are available, and ways that positive engagement of, and involvement in, physical activities is modelled by teachers.

Positive mental health and mindfulness activities are positive approaches to whole school well-being planned to encourage everyone in the school community, both pupils and staff to benefit from and engage in a range of well-being and mindful activities. Do these opportunities meet the needs of staff and pupils or could more be done to recognize what would support staff and pupils most?

Reflective questions

1. Do you, for example, ensure that pupils, even those with physical differences, have regular physical activity breaks? If not, is this a practice issue for you, an environmental difficulty or a lack of understanding about the importance of physical activity?
2. How are sport and physical activities promoted in the school, including in after school, before school, break-time and lunchtime clubs and activities?
3. Do the activities that are available actually match the activities that pupils want to/can participate in? This again is particularly relevant for those pupils with mental health or social skills needs and should be considered by you on an individual basis.
4. How are pupils and teachers in the school supported to understand and recognize the link between physical activity and improvements in positive mental health?

Reflexive questions

1. If you are not finding the time to take physical breaks throughout the day, think carefully about why this might be the case?
2. Have past experiences influenced your teaching practice or are there issues relating to your own physical welfare that again are impacting on your practice?

Implications for educators

We offer no easy solutions, no simple course to attend, or manual to follow. Instead we wish to encourage professional decision-making – difficult though that may be in the current climate. Education settings are complex and reducing that complexity will diminish these unique places and the special role they can play in the lives of children and the those who choose to work with them. Our advice is to gather all the information that you can, from educational literature, practical experience and from the children themselves, and to use this to inform your practice. But we do ask you to recognize your humanity – we are not superheroes who can withstand all that confronts us – and to take time to talk, preferably in a supervisory relationship.

Annotated bibliography

Bainbridge, A., Reid, H. and Del Negro, G. (2019). 'Towards a virtuosity of
school leadership: Clinical support and supervision as professional learning',
Professional Development in Education. **doi:10.1080/19415257.2019.1700152**
This paper introduces an innovative clinical support and supervision project that
has its origins in the concern for how school leaders are increasingly being expected
to manage the escalating demand to care for pupils, families and often the wider
community. The provision of supervision meets the moral obligation to care for
those who care for others in educational settings.

Ekins, A., Robinson, S., Durrant, I. and Summers, K. (2017). *Educating children
with life-limiting conditions.* **Abingdon: Routledge.**
This book, written by a team of both education and health professionals, focuses on
supporting mainstream teachers to understand and positively plan for the complex
and challenging needs of pupils with life-limiting illnesses and conditions. The
emotional impact of this on the staff team themselves, as well as on the child and
other children and parents within the school setting, is examined, with a range of
practical examples and exemplars provided to support positive planning within the
mainstream school context.

4

The Learning Environment

Lorna Hughes and Nicola Elson

What is a learning environment?

In its most simplistic form, the learning environment is the physical space in which learning occurs. However, the myriad of factors impacting upon the environment means this is by no means a simplistic feature when supporting pupils with special and able and talented needs. Basic environmental conditions such as the temperature or lighting can influence learning, even before considering the wider and more complex factors such as social interactions, cultural backgrounds and political agendas. The school timetable, curriculum, access to funds and resources, as well as the operational systems and organizational structures, will impact on the learning environment. If certain learning spaces are only available at certain times of the day or there is a rigid hierarchical system in a school, this will influence the people within the school and therefore the environment for learning. The school is 'part of a wider, dynamic web of cultural and social aspects' (Woolner et al., 2012, p. 46).

Why is the learning environment important?

As a teacher it is important to provide supportive foundations for learning such as the need for safety and security (Maslow, 1954) and the development of a sense of belonging. Lowrey et al. (2017, p. 17) note the 'interrelationship between safety and belonging (emotion) and cognitive development (learning)' when exploring inclusive education and note this as fostering collaboration and a sense of community in pupils. Therefore, you are a key proponent in not only designing and managing the physical area of the learning space, but also in fostering inclusive learning environments through the dominant attitudes, beliefs, language and expectations.

The wider learning environment

You can make decisions over aspects of the learning environment such as change from a formal, structured class to a more informal school trip into the wider community.

Schools are not entities which exist in isolation. The school learning environment is one which is developed based on the context in which it is situated. The pupil and interactions cannot be viewed in isolation and different settings and influences on the learning environment will affect outcomes. Hughes and Pollard (2006, p. 393) acknowledge this difference and that every school and community will be distinctive requiring approaches to be 'tailored to the characteristics of the particular communities served by individual schools'. Consequently, the learning environment is to an extent a reflection of a community and fostering effective communities of learning can lead to the development of effective learning environments.

So, the learning environment does not stop with the physical space, as the learning does not stop with the end of the school day. Learning environments include wider spaces, the community and engagement with parents, which can influence wider outcomes and desires, such as lifelong learning or possibly links to opportunities and engagement in future employment.

Reflective question

The learning environment you create and interact with as teachers may be an important aspect for a pupil's whole life and not just relevant to their school years. Where are you positioned in supporting lifelong learning and which factors can you influence in your practice to impact positively on pupils?

Access and opportunity

Although there are a range of aspects which will influence access and opportunity for pupils with special and able and talented needs, the focus here considers the development and enactment of the curriculum for all pupils (Sustainable Development Goal 4; UNESCO, 2019a). This includes the physical building and the teaching practices (pedagogical approaches) facilitated within different spaces.

The physical buildings and space

You and your pupils may have some autonomy over the physical space, such as where you are positioned, organization of furniture, displays or the creation of specific learning areas. However, resources can be limited and will affect educational opportunities. Only 37 per cent of children educated in upper secondary schools in low-income countries have access to the internet compared with 93 per cent in high-income countries and even basics such as drinking water and sanitation are not universal (UNESCO, 2019b). You may not have direct control over the physical buildings in which you teach, but how you respond to your situation based on your context and the available resources is within your professional capabilities.

Case study: Teaching in community spaces

Country: India

Age group: 5–11 years

Setting: Various community spaces

Participants involved: Volunteer teachers delivering a religious education curriculum

The case study

Non-standard classrooms can present challenges when planning teaching activities. This case study reflects observations of volunteer teachers in a range of different learning environments, including domestic houses, large community halls and small side rooms with few facilities.

Small spaces

Some teaching rooms were not designed as spaces for learning, but often no alternative would be available. One observation took place in a cramped space with just enough room for five or six children to sit on the floor. There was very little natural light and the space was too small for furniture or equipment other than a small white board and laptop. The session was predominantly led by the teacher in the same space for two hours, which ultimately led to children becoming restless and unfocused and begging the question if traditional class approaches work in these spaces.

Large open spaces

Observations of teaching in large community halls could involve one small group of students, or it could include multiple large groups of children being taught different topics in the same space. The high ceilings affected acoustics, making it difficult to hear and, again, there was a lack of resources and furniture because these spaces have not been designed for teaching and learning. On one occasion, the teacher made good use of the space to facilitate group work by sectioning off specific areas to view resources, create and practise presentations, thereby utilizing the potential of the larger space available.

Outcomes

Non-standard classrooms can impact on learning opportunities due to restrictive spaces, limited resources, poor acoustics, little natural light or managing distractions from other groups. However, success was more evident when teachers acknowledged the non-standard environment and planned non-standard lessons and activities.

What we can learn

Considering what is available as opposed to what is not available may be a better approach to teaching in non-standard spaces. Being solution-focused rather than problem finding is always the most positive approach for teachers. When restricted by a small space, using outside spaces for a focused task could add movement opportunities, facilitate group work and aid transitions through the session.

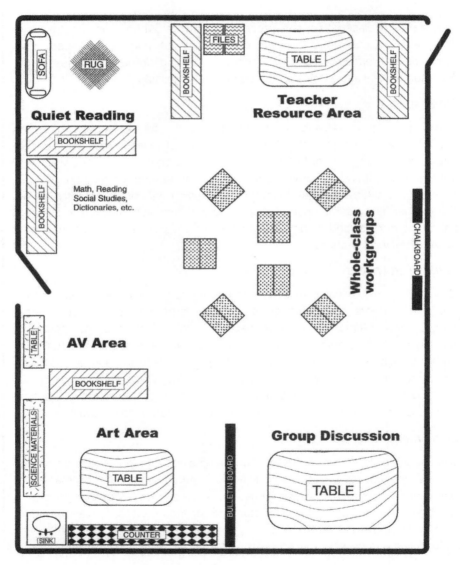

Figure 4.1 Self-contained classroom organized for cooperative learning (Vincent, 1999). Reproduced courtesy of Education Northwest.

Providing clear demarked spaces in large halls can help to set learning zones (e.g. planning zone, resource area, reading area, presentation area etc.) facilitating variety and clear transitions to different activities or aiding multi-grade teaching.

Utilizing community spaces may also foster a more connected community. For example, using the smaller rooms to interview visitors on the topic being studied, or creating a performance to deliver to the community members in larger spaces.

Organization of the physical space and how this is utilized can impact on learning. In Figure 4.1, the space is organized to include different learning areas (such as the 'AV' audio-visual area) and cooperative spaces for learning, but still provides opportunity for some independence with the 'Quiet Reading' area. This is quite different from what might be considered a traditional class layout with desks in rows facing the teacher positioned at the front of the class.

In some cases, trialling new classroom layouts can provide insights into balancing different learning opportunities and the individual pupils' needs. One static learning environment will not meet the needs of all pupils and therefore there is a necessity for a range of learning environments and adaptions. Diversity in the physical space and pedagogy can then meet the diverse needs of pupils. For example, there is value in group work, but also value in independent work, but the same physical learning space may not be wholly suitable for both.

Reflective question

Draw a floorplan of your classroom. Now consider the activities you will be conducting as well as the pupils in your class. Is the physical environment organized in a way to facilitate learning for your situation? Create a new floorplan and discuss with a colleague some of the changes you propose to make to the physical space and what impact you think this may have on learning.

The pedagogical approaches

There may be limitations over the physical space itself, and to an extent your teaching practice and the approaches you adopt will be influenced by this space. Learning environments can be viewed as a 'change agent' (Oblinger, 2006) which interplay dynamically with the teaching and learning process.

Window on research: Transition from a traditional classroom to an innovative learning environment

Byers, Imms and Hartnell-Young (2018) illustrated that innovative learning spaces (e.g. technology enhanced spaces, open learning spaces, flexible areas etc.) can lead to improved engagement, foster collaborative learning and promote less didactic approaches to teaching. Their study explored the introduction of flexible and technology-rich spaces in a secondary boys' school in an Australian city to ascertain if the changed spaces would affect teachers' behaviours and pedagogical approaches.

The societal move from 'industrial to knowledge economies' (Byers, Imms and Hartnell-Young, 2018, p. 156) requires a change in the ways in which our learning environments foster lifelong learners, learner-centred practices, technology-enhanced skills and active constructivist approaches as opposed to more traditional passive, didactic teacher-led approaches; arguably moving pupils from surface to deep learning. The study focused on how the change in learning environment influenced teacher behaviour and the teaching approaches adopted, the types of learning experience encountered, how teachers grouped the pupils, how technology was used and any barriers in relation to using the new spaces.

Their findings supported the notion that rigid physical layout of space (such as a traditional classroom) led to more rigid structures in teaching. In the innovative learning environment, the pedagogical approaches adopted by teachers included pupil-centred approaches which led to more on-task behaviours and pupil autonomy which Byers, Imms and Hartnell-Young (2018) claim are skills pupils require for the twenty-first century. The teachers were observed to include more discussion feedback and questioning. One teacher commented that 'the design "of the workshop spaces made it difficult to just stand in front of a class and talk to them for an extended period"' (ibid., 161).

There were more opportunities for collaborative learning and the formation of learning communities because there was less whole class–led instruction and more group work. This also facilitated better differentiation because traditionally teachers 'appeared to favour either the whole class [work] or students working individually' (Byers, Imms and Hartnell-Young, 2018, p. 163).

Although there was positive evidence for the move to innovative learning environments, barriers were identified, including the time required to adjust to the new spaces as well as the teachers' level of experience in managing this transition. Being faced with an unfamiliar physical space can present as difficult or discomforting for both the teacher and the pupil. Moving to new or different learning environments involves drawing on pedagogical and professional expertise and so the confidence and competence of the teacher in new situations may influence how successfully the change is embraced.

What we can learn

Changes to physical space do not automatically mean the practice within the spaces will change. It may well continue as before without any adjustment (Woolner, 2012). The cultures, ethos and sometimes embedded pedagogical approaches may stay static in a physical environment which has progressed. Essentially, what happens in the space is surely more important than the physical space itself. Mulcahy (2015, p. 511) proposes that it is not important whether the 'concept of space (open, flexible, contained, traditional) is "true" but whether it works, and whether it opens up possibilities'. Some spaces such as large, open learning plazas could present as more challenging for pupils with sensory sensitivities and a more traditional classroom may be preferable. Supporting individuals so the space does 'work' for them and 'opens possibilities' is key.

One framework for developing an inclusive learning environment which aims to optimize learning for all irrespective of the available resources is Universal Design for Learning (UDL) which is based on three key principles:

Engagement: How can I engage all pupils in my class?

Representation: How can I present information in ways that reach all pupils?

Action and Expression: How can I offer purposeful options for pupils to show what they know (understood.org, 2019)?

UDL has been adopted within public policy in the United States and collaborative approaches in implementing UDL could strengthen professional development and resultant inclusive practices.

Reflective question

Consider your current knowledge of inclusive practices in the classroom. How could you use the UDL framework to develop your understanding of inclusive practice? Use this developed understanding to plan a more inclusive learning environment for your pupils.

The outdoor environment

Consideration of a conducive learning environment, however, should extend far beyond the four walls of the classroom and indeed the school building itself. Sutherland and Gosteva (2019, p. 33) acknowledge that 'play and playgrounds are critical for children's social and communication development'. The opportunities offered to pupils via outdoor learning are well documented across all areas of development including physical, emotional, social, cognitive and creative.

Why is the outdoor environment important?

When you are planning for the curriculum to be delivered beyond the classroom, it is particularly significant for both pupils with special educational needs, as well as pupils with a dual and/or multiple exceptionality (DME). Pupils may benefit from a more practical, kinaesthetic or multi-sensory teaching approach than that typically experienced within the classroom. No matter how small the outdoor learning environment available within a setting, it will usually afford more physical space than that offered within the typical classroom, undeterred by the physical boundaries of walls, chairs, tables and equipment. Consequently, for pupils with a special educational need or a DME who do not necessarily require *desk-based* teaching, the outdoor environment offers opportunities for more practical, holistic, as well as real-life learning experiences (Austin, 2007).

Outdoor learning has been shown to be beneficial for a broad range of additional learning needs. In their study exploring assessment in the early years' outdoor classroom, Davies and Hamilton (2018) observed that an outdoor environment particularly suited pupils with language difficulties or delayed social development. Positive impact included increased independence and social opportunities, with a more conducive environment to develop language skills. Likewise, according to Etherington (2012), pupils on the autism spectrum may appear calmer outside in a more natural sensory environment whilst a positive impact has similarly been noted for pupils with ADHD, including improved self-esteem, behaviour and relationships (Neenan and Knight, 2012).

Positive benefits of outdoor learning environments have also been noted among able and talented pupils. Maciver (2012), for example, observed a group of pupils aged five to seven years participate in a Forest School project in which challenge and extension were fostered. The open-ended learning approach encouraged pupils to develop their interests and set their own challenges after which pupils were noted to have grown in both confidence and leadership skills. This has implications particularly for pupils with a DME and who may be talented in practical, creative and craft-based areas and thus preferring a more individualized approach.

Extending the learning environment beyond the classroom

How then can you adapt the learning environment to facilitate learning and inclusion for special and able and talented pupils?

Within the school grounds

Adapting the curriculum and planning for learning opportunities within the school grounds may simply involve delivering a literacy lesson sat on the grass outside, or developing numeracy skills incorporating, for example, data collection whilst classifying wildlife. Science can be enhanced by fieldwork activities, for example studying plants, animals and habitats as well as physical geographic features including the weather and seasons. Malone and Waite (2016) refer to studies in America where experiential education in the natural environment for subjects such as science has led to significant gains in test scores. Other curriculum subjects could similarly incorporate the outdoors as a vehicle for teaching and learning including outdoor art, making bird boxes in Design and Technology or extending Physical Education to include orienteering or a nature treasure hunt.

Cross-curricular activities can similarly maximize outdoor learning opportunities. For example, the simple activity of growing tomatoes can facilitate learning in science (plant growth), numeracy (data recording – e.g. days and height), literacy (report writing) and Design and Technology (cooking soup), alongside the development of fine motor skills (chopping vegetables) and communication and social skills (undertaking a science research project in pairs or small teams). Even in limited school grounds it should be possible for you to extend learning activities outside of the classroom with dedicated curriculum planning.

Reflective question

How can you improve on your existing practice to provide a learning environment that offers access to a range of opportunities for learning beyond the classroom walls?

Reflexive question

Consider carefully if your own personal beliefs, experiences and values influence your engagement with an 'outdoor' curriculum?

Within the community

Learning takes place beyond the school grounds including both within the local environment and further afield. This includes not just the outdoors, as such, but all locations outside of the classroom. You may plan direct, experiential learning in a wide range of environments including, for example, places of worship, heritage sites, theatres and farms. Participation in cultural festivals, camps and sports events can facilitate increased engagement levels whilst building bridges between theory and reality. As well as supporting social and emotional development, learning within the local community offers the opportunity for pupils to develop a range of personal, social, citizenship and life skills, including shopping, travel training and work experience.

Wider environmental issues

The recent surge of heightened interest in wider global issues has further highlighted the need for increased awareness of the outdoor environment. In 2015, the United Nations (2019a) outlined its seventeen sustainable development goals which featured several environmental issues including action to combat climate change alongside conservation and sustainability of land and oceans. Thus, considering lesson planning, the use of resources and the emotional responses of the pupils is crucial when wider environmental issues are incorporated into curriculum planning.

> ## Reflexive question
>
> How would you plan to incorporate 'environmental awareness' into your curriculum and encourage pupils with learning differences to become more socially responsible whilst developing their 'global' citizenship skills?

The community

Engagement and involvement in society are instrumental factors throughout school life, but also beyond school. The ways in which transitions are managed by drawing on the support of wider communities, including the support of parents, can facilitate success beyond formal school years.

The interactive nature of the learning environment and the factors which come into play are important when considering pupil-centred approaches to supporting transitions through an educational journey. You will be aware that for your individual pupils this could be very different; sometimes immediate family members relocate for work; sometimes children are raised by extended family; sometimes the personal, cultural or political circumstances can impact on wider family support. Yet, children in all communities should be at the centre of shaping their learning experiences 'guided by the abilities and values that are important in their culture' (Couper and Sutherland, 2019, p. 118) to successfully develop as individuals.

The power of parents

Parents and carers are integral to their child's education and are foundational to the mesosystem and beyond (Bronfenbrenner, 1979). They can be powerful advocates in supporting and directly influencing successful outcomes especially for pupils with special educational needs, DME, or gifts and talents. However, building relationships with parents that are effective can present challenges as well as benefits. Hughes and Pollard (2006, p. 388) consider the school's relationship with the community and ways to foster effective parental engagement in their Home–School Knowledge Exchange Project. They acknowledge that 'attempts to increase parental involvement often amount in practice to attempts to impose school-favoured values and behaviour on less advantaged families'. In a way to address this imbalance, they utilized 'funds of knowledge' (Moll and Greenberg, 1990) to support a collaborative approach which does not 'favour' a particular position but draws on the value of the teachers' knowledge and the parents' knowledge and how this can facilitate improved learning conditions. There is real value in this wider knowledge and often times teachers and school may be 'unaware of the funds of knowledge in the communities of their students' (Hughes and Pollard, 2006, p. 388). By drawing on the collaborative knowledge of parents and schools, it provides a strengthened foundation for supporting pupils from diverse backgrounds and supporting their individual needs.

Virtual learning

The relationship with parents will present as a physical community that can often visit school, interact directly and be present. However, communities also include virtual representation through media technologies providing opportunities 'for creativity, for community and for self-fulfilment' (Buckingham, 2000, p. 41). In some contexts, you will be balancing the learning environment so there is opportunity to engage with technology as well as the natural environment. Couper and Sutherland (2019, p. 22) question the move away from learning and play in school playgrounds because 'children are spending more and more time inside than any previous generation'. Advances in technology can provide your pupils with powerful tools for learning which takes them beyond the physical space. Increasing access to tablets, laptops and smartphones provides quick access to the internet and the potential for innovation in working with wider communities of learners, but it is important you consider the limitations as well as the benefits because there is real value in direct interaction too (see Chapter 5 for more information).

Transitions beyond school

Support for transitions to new learning environments is important for all pupils, but this can present more challenge for individuals with learning differences. Transitions within school (a new teacher, classroom, structure to the day) present as challenging and so transitioning to a new educational setting or community can be overwhelming without the right preparation and support. Elson (2011) identified inconsistencies with information sharing at transition from school to further education, thereby recognizing the crucial role of the teacher in ensuring pupils are appropriately prepared and supported when moving beyond formal schooling is essential.

You also need to consider longer-term implications for your pupils, as some may transition to higher education or take up other learning opportunities as adults. Lambe et al. (2019) explored the perspectives of pupils with autism who transitioned to university due to their higher attrition rates. Without appropriate support, the change in environment was highlighted as a factor which can lead to pupils perceiving the failing as their own.

As teachers it is important not only to ensure pupils are prepared for the changes they may face in school, but also to consider their future journey into new situations as adults. Understanding that changes to ensure better access for pupils with autism, or indeed any other individual differences including those who are high academically or creatively achieving, will ultimately enrich the learning experiences of others. Inclusive practices adopted within the learning environment and appreciating that 'there is no one-size-fits-all' (Lambe et al., 2019, p. 1539) reinforce our position in supporting pupils as they progress beyond our physical learning environment.

Reflective questions

1. Consider a pupil with a special educational need or another learning difference who is in the process of transitioning into or out of your school setting. How do you respond effectively to their individual needs by planning possible approaches and adaptions to the new environment they will be entering?
2. What do you think is your responsibility as a teacher socially, emotionally and professionally?

Reflexive question

How do your own experiences and values influence your practice decisions when carrying out transitioning planning?

Employment

Preparation for the world of work should ultimately be one of the fundamental aims of all education systems, and hence for every teacher. It should not only prepare young people to be able to contribute to society at large but also ensure that they are able to be engaged in meaningful activity. However, Dillenburger et al. (2019, p. 11) assert that 'people with disabilities are disproportionately unemployed or under-employed'. Possible reasons for exclusion from the workplace include a lack of marketable skills and potential prejudice or a lack of understanding from employers (Skellern and Astbury, 2012). If you can challenge and possibly overcome this in the learning environment, the potential benefits of employment are paramount including not only a pathway to social inclusion (Skellern and Astbury, 2012) but also positive effects on well-being, physical and mental health (DoH, 2009).

Reflexive question

What drives your thinking and action when reflecting on your responsibility towards preparation for life and employment?

Reflective question

Regardless of the age and need type of your pupils, how can you incorporate opportunities to develop work-based skills and responsibilities into your curriculum?

Implications in schools and colleges

Work-based learning

What are the implications, therefore, for educators? In England, the *Special Educational Needs and Disability code of practice* (DfE and DoH, 2014, 2015) advocates work-based learning and first-hand experience of the world of work as being one of the most effective means of preparation for employment for young people with SEN. As well as pathways such as apprenticeships and traineeships for older pupils, an increasingly popular initiative is that of *supported internships*. Based on the *supported employment* model originating in the United States in the 1990s (Skellern and Astbury, 2012) and as an alternative to sheltered workshops (Dillenburger et al., 2019), pupils follow a structured and personalized study programme which incorporates extended, unpaid work placements with an employer and typically supported by a *Job Coach* (DfE and DoH, 2015).

You need to consider the ways in which your pupils and the lessons you teach relate to the future skills required in employment. This could be exposure to occupations related to the area of study or planning enterprising elements with project work. Essentially, preparation for adulthood is of crucial importance and the curriculum in your school/college or setting can embed the required knowledge and skills, including consideration of alternative pathways for those pupils unlikely to follow the more traditional academic routes.

Work experience programmes

Several schools and colleges have very successfully developed their own internal vocational programmes alongside or in place of more formal work-based learning programmes. Numerous smaller-scale *enterprise* initiatives can easily be delivered within the school curriculum incorporating a range of employability skills such as design, production, marketing, advertising and sales as well as more generic skills such as money handling, communication and teamwork. Seasonal fetes such as the annual Christmas or Summer Fete or a weekly *Friday Market* offer a wealth of opportunities for pupils to develop retail skills, producing and selling a range of craft items, school-grown plants and vegetables as well as school fare such as cakes and jam!

Cafe-style events can also offer opportunities to develop hospitality and service skills such as serving drinks and foods. UNICEF Jamaica (2016) celebrates the *Deaf Can! Coffee* enterprise in Jamaica in which young people who are deaf embarked upon a *Coffee* enterprise within their school setting. This has now grown into a full-fledged cafe, illustrating the scope of such enterprises to offer vocational and employment opportunities for special and able and talented pupils. As a teacher you can utilize such approaches to teaching and learning as a conscious decision by yourself to prepare pupils for employment through problem-solving skills, interpersonal skills and financial understanding. Additional daily jobs such as that of register monitor, Physical Education assistant or school postman, particularly suitable for younger pupils, can also begin to instil and teach pupils of all ages about the responsibilities and satisfactions of work.

Case study: Vocational learning programme

Country: UK

Age group: 14–25 years

Setting: St John's School and College is a non-maintained special school and independent specialist college in the south-east of England catering for young people aged 7–25 years with complex learning disabilities, autistic spectrum conditions and social, emotional and mental health needs.

Participants involved: Teacher

The case study

Review of the school's vocational programme

Outcomes

Whilst one of its core values is to enable pupils to realize their potential and prepare for adulthood and life beyond school and college, this is underpinned by a philosophy and curriculum emphasis on employability alongside independence, well-being, communication and skills. Pupils at the school engage in a wide range of enterprise projects, including running stands at local markets and delivering flowers to local dementia homes, whilst older pupils follow an individualized vocational programme which incorporates 'real-life' and hands-on work ventures. These include a number of initiatives including:

Horticulture	*Flourish* incorporates grounds and horticulture, cultivating and preparing plants to sell in the community and maintaining the outdoor spaces
Catering and Hospitality	*Scrummies*, a cafe and delicatessen, in which pupils prepare and serve breakfast, lunch and hot drinks and learn to operate professional dishwashing and laundry equipment
Maintenance	*Foundations*, the maintenance team, developing skills in painting, decorating, carpentry, electrical work and construction
Administration	*Solutions*, the stationery and administration department, in which students learn how to operate industry-standard stationery production as well as working on Reception
Technology	*abil.it.y*, the technology department – pupils learn how to maintain and repair IT equipment as well as generate content for digital use, such as social media posts and online multimedia productions
Print	*Inklusion Print*, a dedicated social enterprise producing a variety of products including canvas prints, clothing, mugs and cards, supported by '*Inklusion Studio*' where the designs are created
Retail	*Inspirations*, a retail enterprise, selling a variety of items such as mugs, wrapping paper and T-shirts

What we can learn

St John's achieves this unique vocational curriculum by linking the central functions and services of the organization with the learning that is provided each day in its curriculum throughout the school and college.

Alongside learning specific practical skills, pupils also develop generic skills such as packaging and labelling products and merchandizing stock in preparation for working in real working environments, such as at their *pop-up* shops within the community. External work experience placements with, for example, supermarket chains and local theatres provide supplementary opportunities to develop key employability skills such as time keeping, appropriate dress and behaviour and following instructions from employers.

Alternative options

It is important to highlight, however, that *paid* employment in adulthood may not be feasible for all. Hall and Wilton (2011, p. 868) stress that 'for many ... the transition into employment is fraught with difficulties, from finding and gaining a job, to relations within the workplace and securing a living wage'. Alternative options, including volunteering, creative arts projects and social enterprise initiatives, could offer positive work and social participation opportunities, whilst facilitating scope to develop self-confidence and further enhancing skills. As asserted by Hall and Wilton (2011, p. 874), 'Voluntary work is a socially-valued activity, with both individual and community benefit.' By ensuring that all pupils can participate as fully as they are able to in these types of enterprising and creative activities, you will hopefully support more positive lifelong outcomes.

Reflective question

How do or could you accommodate the (sometimes contrasting) needs of all stakeholders, including, for example, pupils, parents, employers and other professional staff, when considering post-school options for your pupils?

Conclusion

The learning environment can significantly impact upon the level of engagement and learning of pupils and it is imperative, therefore, that plans and measures are put into place to ensure that the environment matches the specific needs of all pupils with special educational needs or who are able, gifted and/or talented. This should include consideration for pupils at all age phases from early years through to post-compulsory education alongside the broader areas of environment including the classroom setting, curriculum design, the structure of the school building, the outdoor environment and the wider community.

In many countries, teachers are obliged to uphold their country's own professional Teachers' Standards which will usually include reference to the learning environment. The standards in both England and Australia, for example, highlight that teachers need to be creating supportive, safe and stimulating learning environments (aitsl, 2011; DfE, 2011). However, attaining professional standards does not end upon initial qualification into the teaching profession but rather begins. Although Continuing Professional Development (CPD) is crucial and may include further specific training in relation to teaching either special and/or able and talented learners, the learning environment itself, and also your own personal beliefs, values and experiences are equally important.

As a teacher what do you personally, socially and emotionally need to consider? Consider your professional responsibilities:

- Personal responsibility – reflecting upon and having self-awareness of your own personal views of the learning environment and your response to CPD opportunities. What is your opinion of being a lifelong learner?
- Social responsibility – respecting and utilizing resources both indoors and outdoors and considering your own values in relation to providing learning opportunities in the wider community.
- Emotional responsibility – reflecting upon how to respond effectively when experiencing different issues within the environment. Consider your personal views as well as consideration of the opinions of others regarding the development of inclusive learning environments.

This chapter has shown that the broader learning environment is a significant aspect for a person's whole life, not only during the school years, but also beyond into adulthood. The teacher's role, therefore, as well as their thinking and practice in these areas, are of crucial importance.

Annotated bibliography

Austin, R. (ed.) (2007). *Letting the outside in – Developing teaching and learning beyond the early years' classroom.* **Stoke on Trent: Trentham Books Limited.**
Practical guidance on creatively enhancing the learning environment to address some of the restrictions teachers might face from 'traditional' schooling. There is a focus on four main areas; the links between school and a child's homelife; the physical learning environment; the adults' role in developing children's learning and how the needs of the individual are balanced against a standard curriculum. Each of these areas is explored through a range of authors' perspectives in different subject areas and contexts from exploring children's physical needs and movement to developing their understanding of ecological principles.

Couper, L. and Sutherland, D. (2019). *Learning and connecting in school playgrounds: Using the playground as a curriculum resource.* **Abingdon: Routledge.**
Places the importance on play as a medium for children's well-being and development as well as a way in which to enhance their learning opportunities. The playground and positive play experiences are explored including the valuable social and emotional aspects, such as developing a sense of belonging and self-confidence as

well as physical health benefits for children. Examples from practice are explored by the authors to present how the playground can be effectively fostered as a curriculum resource in school settings.

Woolner, P., McCarter, S., Wall, K. and Higgins, S. (2012). 'Changed learning through changed space. When can a participatory approach to the learning environment challenge perceptions and alter practice?', *Improving Schools*, 15(1), pp. 45–60.

This article presents case study research on teachers' and children's perspectives of their learning spaces. Physical space can sometime entrench certain practices and approaches. However, making changes to the physical space in schools does not necessarily mean there will be subsequent changes to pedagogical approaches. The authors consider the benefits of participatory models for the design and development of effective learning spaces.

5
Technology
John-Paul Riordan and Mark Roberts

Introduction

Technology in twenty-first-century education is important for all pupils, but it can be crucial for those pupils who have additional physical, sensory or academic needs. This chapter will, therefore, provide an overview of technology available for enhancing access to learning for those with special educational needs (SEN), disabilities, or those who are particularly academically able or have a dual or multiple exceptionality (DME) (Montgomery, 2015). It will explore how technology can impact learning in classrooms and suggest how the use of technology in school to support learning could develop in the future. It seeks to help teachers make their classrooms more technologically inclusive for all pupils.

Assistive and inclusive technology

Effective use of technology in school involves assessing users' needs and selecting appropriate and available devices. It is crucial to seek proactively and find professional help with these issues. It is also vital to get training in how devices should be used, and maintained, to meet individual pupils' needs.[1] Furthermore, users and their families are a key source of information regarding their current technology and technological skills.

Discussion about technology and inclusion in education often uses the term **assistive technology**, defined as:

> Any product, instrument, equipment or technology adapted or specially designed for improving the functioning of a person with disability.
>
> (Borg, Larsson and Östergren, 2011, pp. 153–4)

---

[1] Here technology refers to the use of scientific knowledge for practical purposes within education.

However, it is perhaps more important to think about the term '**inclusive technology**' (Hayhoe, 2014). This refers to generally available technology which is preferable to specialist assistive technology because it is usually widely available, less expensive and more familiar to users, their families and teachers.

Context

Teachers always need to remember their responsibilities for ensuring that all pupils they teach have technology which not only facilitates but fully enables strengths and potential. Access to technology (and the services necessary for effective delivery) can be considered a human right (Borg, Larsson and Östergren, 2011; United Nations, 2007) and is vital for the world economy. Individual countries also have their specific policies and legislation concerning technology and those pupils with learning differences. The UK Equality Act (2010), for example, obliges service providers not to discriminate against people with disabilities because of their disability, and the SEND code of practice (DfE and DoH, 2015) in England maintains that all schools must ensure pupils get all necessary support and resources. The UK Equality Act (2010) is referenced in the SEND code of practice (pp. 16 and 38) and is broken down in terms of the legal obligations that early years providers, schools, post-16 institutions and local authorities have. There is much excellent inclusive practice in all parts of the UK and other parts of Europe (Armstrong, Armstrong and Barton, 2016), yet as evidenced in a recent report by the United Nations Committee on the Rights of Persons with Disabilities, 'systematic violations' of the rights of disabled people in the UK, including in education, are still far too common (OHCHR, 2016). The UK is not alone in this, and in some parts of the world, education for people with special educational needs particularly remains inadequate or unavailable (Ainscow and César, 2006). Inclusive technology helps teachers to address this issue directly, by ensuring careful consideration of children's needs so that appropriate resources to support learning and inclusion will be selected.

Reflexive question: Starting points

What experiences do you have of inclusion, exclusion, integration and segregation (see Figure 5.1)? Consider how these experiences have influenced you and hence your professional practice.

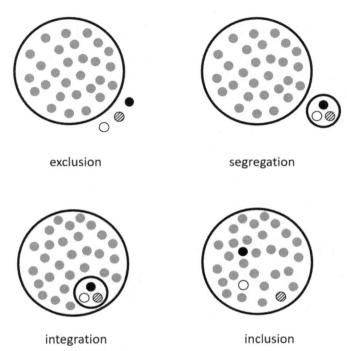

exclusion   segregation

integration   inclusion

Figure 5.1 Illustration of inclusion, exclusion, integration and segregation (adapted from the United Nations Committee on the Rights of Persons with Disabilities general comment no. 4 and cited in Hehir et al., 2016).

Appropriate use of technology

Access to appropriate technology, at the right time, can help develop pupils' independence and agency. However, it is quite likely the user and educators will need skills training to enable this to happen (Alper and Raharinirina, 2006). Few initial teacher education courses include specific training on assistive technology, but this is crucial if inclusive practice is going to continue advancing (Todis, 1996). The input during courses could be more precisely targeted by recognizing inclusive technology currently available and whatever technology may already be being used by pupils and their families.

Reflective questions: Personal responsibility

1. What is the extent of your responsibility as an educator, and that of colleagues, for helping pupils' access to appropriate technology?
2. How do you feel about this, especially when considering challenging aspects of technology (e.g. online bullying, gaming addiction etc.)?

Technology for teaching and learning

There are hundreds of different devices used in different ways by pupils with SEN around the world. Technological change is as rapid in education as in the rest of society. Using technology in lessons involves identifying what technologies are available (means), how such devices might be used (strategy), estimating what learning could be achieved (ends), finding out who knows what (information, misinformation and disinformation) and dealing with things going awry (accidents) (Riordan, 2020). It is important to remember that the use of technology in all aspects of teaching and learning can aid the highly academically able who might need additional and different emotional and social support. This is discussed in greater detail later on in the chapter.

Classifying technology

Technology may be categorized by its level of sophistication (Mitchell, 2007). Low-technology devices are generally not electronic (e.g. pencil grips, reading stands etc.). Medium technology involves simple electronics (e.g. a video camera) and high technology uses complex digital devices or software (e.g. a smartphone). An alternative classification is by the needs of potential beneficiaries. The following sections summarize some important technologies associated with particular areas of need, directing you to research literature for further information. This summary is not comprehensive but aims to encourage questions about the availability of technology and its potential use to support learning.

People with physical differences

You will likely need to think about meeting the needs of a pupil with a physical difference in your class or school. People with physical differences can use a huge variety of aids. Mobility aids range from ancient low-technology solutions like a walking stick to the latest robotic prosthetic. There are many things to think about to ensure a pupil with a physical difference feels and is included in a classroom. You will probably immediately consider physical changes to the learning environment such as adapting the workspace appropriately (e.g. table height, wrist support etc.). Computer operating systems have inbuilt adjustment options (e.g. Windows 10 'sticky keys' avoids users having to hold down a modifier key like 'shift') and these can be tailored to the user. The device itself may need physical modification (e.g. the Xbox adaptive controller or a rollerball mouse) to become accessible. In addition to learning tools, aids supporting daily living may also be required. These range from low-technology devices like an adapted pen grip, to high-technology solutions like a virtual assistant on a smartphone controlling a home, school or work environment (e.g. if you have a relatively recent iPhone, you might try saying, 'Hey Siri, turn the torch on'). Comprehensively reviewing this field is beyond our scope, but Murchland and Parkyn (2010) explore experiences of pupils with physical differences who use assistive technology. Additionally, pupils with physical differences frequently encounter difficulties using playgrounds which have not been adapted to meet their needs (Moore and Lynch, 2015). Perhaps your school could do more to make your playground and the physical environment more inclusive? Visiting your local special school could be helpful to see what they do and to share good practice.

Case study: Using eye-gaze technology with pupils with Duchenne Muscular Dystrophy (DMD)

Country: UK

Age group: 15+ years

Setting: One special school in England. People with Duchenne Muscular Dystrophy experience progressive loss of gross and fine motor function over time. Maintaining their ability to use computer technology enhances independence and enables access to a range of supportive software. Initially, pupils were using a single finger on a small trackpad to control both the mouse on the computer and the on-screen keyboard. Set-up required support, and this technology was tiring to use.

Participants involved: Three

Trial

An eye-gaze–enabled computer was set up on a stand, and configured to allow the eye-gaze to control the mouse. The software used the familiar on-screen keyboard. The intention was to allow the pupils to drive up to and independently access the computer, with no need for additional one-to-one support. The aim was to reduce the fatigue of the pupils.

Outcomes

Independent initial calibration was challenging for the pupils. Despite the pupils being good power chair users, they were unable to consistently position themselves accurately to access the eye-gaze technology, and even when they did the system still required further calibration. This meant that initial set-up support was still required.

What we can learn

The pupils were easily able to use the technology, which they found engaging and encouraging. However, they still experienced fatigue as the concentration and eye control required meant that they could not use the system for prolonged periods.

People with sensory impairments
Visual impairment

Over 2.2 billion people worldwide have a visual impairment or blindness (WHO, 2019) and therefore it is important to think about people with this need in your classrooms. For example, the adjustment of lighting in school can help some (Mitchell, 2007). Many children and adults experience visual stress and adapting the learning environment lighting to suit them can make a huge difference. Table 5.1 provides you with several ideas and suggestions to aid pupils with a visual need in the school environment.

Auditory impairment

Approximately 6.1 per cent of people worldwide (466 million people) live with severe hearing loss (WHO, 2018). The number of sign languages worldwide is about 144 (a subset of the 7,111 known living languages) (Ethnologue, 2019). Sign languages are possibly the most widespread technology worldwide used by people with auditory impairment and by those who interact with them. Deuchar (2013) estimated 40,000 people in the UK use British Sign Language (BSL). Pupils with auditory impairments could require different technologies due not only to their sensory differences but to their cognitive abilities as well.

Table 5.1 Technology supporting people with visual impairments

Type of technology	Benefits
Optical devices, e.g. glasses Electronic devices, e.g. Prodigi Connect 12	Enlarges written materials
Braille printers (e.g. Juliet 120) Embossed printing from a standard laser printer (e.g. Touchable Ink)	Prints Braille from a Braille keyboard
Computer and smartphone accessibility settings (e.g. Windows 10 'ease of access' settings)	Allows screen adaptations (e.g. colour customization for pupils with any of the four types of colour blindness)
Talking tactile tablets (also BLITAB tactile tablet)	Audio and haptic information from a tablet computer
Echolocation on smartwatches (Thaler and Goodale, 2016)	Can supplement the use of a white stick
Optical Character Recognition (OCR) devices, e.g. 'Seeing AI' app on an iPhone	Scans writing, recognizes words and then reads aloud the text. Other features include using AI for face, currency, colour and image recognition.
Braille chess Balls which make a sound	Leisure aids for chess and sport
DoorwayOnline	Touch typing learning tool

Technologies used by school pupils with auditory impairments include hearing aids (with or without a loop), cochlear implants, headphones, sound amplification and/or modulation, and visual alarms. Smartphones and computers offer adaptations designed for users with hearing impairments (e.g. Windows 10 ease of access 'closed captions' setting). YouTube allows automatic captioning on live-stream videos. Live transcription is possible using a free app like 'Otter.ai'.

People with speech, language and/or communication difficulties (SLCD)

About 1.2 per cent of people struggle to communicate without help (Bloomberg and Johnson, 1990). Alternative communication devices replace speech or writing, whereas augmentative means supplementing existing capabilities (Costantino and Bonati, 2014). Augmentative and Alternative Communication (AAC) is a subset of assistive technology defined earlier. AAC can be divided into unaided (like signing) and aided (involving external equipment).[2]

Selecting and implementing appropriate AAC interventions for people with SLCD is challenging, but possible, and we would advise close collaboration with specialist support, including from Speech and Language Therapists and Occupational Therapists. Guidelines for selecting appropriate AAC devices are available (Van der Meer et al., 2011), but interventions should not be introduced without close multi-disciplinary working which must include the family. While some educators and parents are concerned that AAC devices might hinder speech acquisition, research shows this is untrue (Light and McNaughton, 2012). For more on technology and people with SLCD see Perelmutter, McGregor and Gordon (2017).

The sign and symbol programme called Makaton is used by more than 100,000 people in over forty different countries (Devarakonda, 2012) and has gained significant influence in the UK in part due to its high-profile use on BBC television (e.g. on the CBeebies programme 'Something Special' with the character of Mr Tumble). It is used by pupils with SLCD and those who support them. Hand gestures are derived from the language of the local deaf community (BSL in the UK). Each sign has an associated symbol, a carefully designed black-and-white line drawing. A core vocabulary of 450 concepts is augmented by a resource vocabulary of about 20,000 concepts. Makaton supports spoken language, so signs and symbols are used with speech and in spoken word order (see Figure 5.2).

It needs only hand gestures and hand-drawn or printed symbols but can be augmented using software or apps like My Choice Pad, a Makaton symbol choice board iPad app. Press a symbol and the iPad speaks the associated word (a longer

---

[2] 'Examples of aided AAC include low-tech communication boards (Sigafoos and Iacono, 1993), picture-exchange (PE) systems (Bondy and Frost, 1994, 2001), and speech-generating devices (SGD), often referred to as voice-output communication aids (VOCA, Lancioni et al., 2007)' (Van der Meer et al., 2011, p. 1423).

to learn (symbol)   to learn (sign)

Figure 5.2 Makaton sign and symbol for 'to learn' © Makaton Charity 2020 (used with permission).

press brings up a video of someone signing). This paid app can be personalized and is useful as a dictionary of Makaton symbols and signs. Makaton symbols can also be used to help pupils who have other needs. For example, some researchers suggest that communication difficulties are the most significant problem for people with autism and that symbols can help. This is discussed more later on in this chapter. Additionally, pupils with behavioural difficulties can benefit from symbol use, since symbols can communicate emotions before, during and after incidents where a pupil might be struggling with their emotional volatility.

Case study: Upgrading communication software

Country: UK

Age group: 5 years

Setting: One Special School in England

Participants involved: One

Example

A pupil who is non-verbal had been provided with a Voice Output Communication Aid (VOCA), accessed through an eye-gaze bar mounted at the base of the VOCA and mounted on their wheelchair. With a basic communication package, this pupil had made good progress using the device. They were confident with good support at home where family members used the device alongside the pupil. Professionals assessing communication progress agreed that the pupil was ready for an upgrade to the software, to give them access to a wider range of vocabulary. They hoped that this would support the pupil's progress.

Outcomes

When the software was upgraded the pupil lost interest in using the VOCA and no longer wanted to use it within the family setting. They chose to use their

> communication book unless they were specifically directed to use the VOCA for communication, which they would then do reluctantly.

What we can learn

While the pupil had been present at the professional discussion, and asked about the changes proposed, the fact that the pupil had not welcomed the changes was not taken into account. While it was the intention to develop the pupils' communication, and the upgrade offered greater opportunities to do this, the readiness of the pupil was not taken into account. As teachers, we have to consider our social, emotional and professional responsibilities to the pupil and their family. We demonstrate this through our actions and decisions with regards to which resources are introduced and how support is provided.

People with learning difficulties

This section will discuss sign and symbol support, literacy and mathematics difficulties, organizational supports, and leisure technologies, for pupils experiencing learning difficulties (LD).

Makaton can also be extremely useful for many people with LD and those who interact with them. Printed symbols are often used in special schools and home environments as some people can point to a symbol as a means of communication.[3] The 'transparency' of the symbol set matters (i.e. the ease with which the symbol can be recognized and the lack of ambiguity in the symbols used). 'Communicate in Print 3' from Widgit is useful for producing printed symbols. Many pupils use communication boards with letters, symbols and/or pictures (e.g. Picture Exchange Communications System (PECS)). Alternatively, a high-technology approach enables users to engage with a symbolized word processor both inside and outside the classroom on a horizontal interactive display (e.g. SymWriter 2 on a HERO Interactive Tilt and Touch Table).[4]

Technology to support literacy for pupils with LD includes electronic worksheets, practice software and websites, abbreviation expanders (e.g. Gus TalkTablet, SpeechWatch) and tactile technology (e.g. tactile letters on Velcro). Many pupils find mathematics challenging, and for some it might help to identify a specific learning difficulty (SpLD) when selecting the most beneficial technology. Dyscalculia and associated pedagogies are discussed in depth by Chinn (2018).

Technology helps pupils with LD with their organization (e.g. a picture or symbol graphic organizer, calendar or schedule, symbolized task lists, symbolized instructions

---

[3] 'Matt' lamination is better than 'glossy' as some children, particularly some people with autism, can find a shiny surface distracting.

[4] See Müller-Tomfelde (2010) for more on horizontal interactive displays.

etc.) and in developing their understanding of time and sequencing. A personal and/ or whole-class visual timer which is not reliant on the user being able to understand numbers can help develop these wider skills. Pupils with LD can benefit from the ability to programme a smartphone using the voice and Siri or Google Assistant (e.g. start and stop a countdown timer, set and stop an alarm, turn a torch on and off, write and send a text, or search the internet). An iPhone can be programmed so that dragging three fingers down any screen starts a screen reader (please search online for instructions for how to turn on the 'enhanced voice option'). Smartphones can have profound effects on the autonomy of pupils with LD and are often used extensively at home as well. School policies which stop pupils with LD from using their smartphone in school may prevent them from learning valuable skills in a supported and safe environment and from accessing the technology which is most familiar to them. It may also prevent them from generalizing skills from one situation to another. We understand that use of mobile phones in schools can lead to difficulties and safeguarding issues, but school may be the best place for pupils (and especially those with LD) to learn to use these devices in intelligent and socially responsible ways.

Smartphones allow voice-controlled audio and video recording (including the ability to vary the speed and other aspects of the sound), audio and video interaction (through voice or video calls, and voice messaging), and speaking apps (e.g. talking calculator). Leisure activities for people with LD can be supported using technology like adapted toys, board games and computer games, accessible websites, or switches like BIGmac (which are effective for sharing information between school and home). Assistive technologies used by and with pupils with LD were reviewed by Adam and Tatnall (2017). For a review of the literature about video games and children with SEN see Durkin et al. (2015).

Reflective questions: Encouraging independence

1. How do you ensure that you actively support and encourage independence for those with organizational/short-term memory needs?
2. In what ways does technology help you achieve this?
3. How might you prepare pupils better for future employment and social interactions?

Pupils with autism

Pupils with autism may have SEN, be very able or have DME. Depending on the academic, social and emotional needs of the individual, technology such as a social skills app (e.g. the Beyond Words Story App) might be appropriate. Supporting people with autism in finding suitable resources to help address their needs, with appropriate support at the right time, can be vital at all stages of life (Boser, Goodwin and Wayland, 2014).

The TEACCH programme for pupils with autism is an evidence-based intervention (Mesibov and Shea, 2010) using many technologies already discussed in this chapter (e.g. visual timetables). The acronym stands for Teaching, Expanding (services), Appreciating (people with autism and their culture), Collaborating and Cooperating (with colleagues, other professionals, people on the autism spectrum and their families), and Holistic (i.e. taking into account the person, their family and the community). TEACCH has behaviourist routes and, like any intervention, should be used with caution (see Tutt, Powell and Thornton, 2006, for a critical discussion). Similarly, AR and Google Glasses together (see the Empower Me system from Brain Power), and therapeutic robots have been used to support pupils with autism.

Pupils with behavioural, emotional or social difficulties

Technologies which may be helpful to consider when supporting pupils with behavioural difficulties include self-regulation tools (e.g. iPrompts), countdown timers or alarms for 'thinking time', calming objects and fidget toys (see Sensoryplus), and emotional awareness or communication software (e.g. Smart Alex). Extrinsic motivation software (e.g. Class Dojo), also called positive behaviour interventions and support (PBIS), can sometimes help (Robacker, Rivera and Warren, 2016), though this will depend upon wider whole-school approaches being open to this technology to be effective. Improving communication skills appears to reduce behavioural difficulties for some children (Law, Plunkett and Stringer, 2012).

The literature on using technology to support pupils with behavioural difficulties was reviewed by Slovák and Fitzpatrick (2015) and provides a useful starting point. Like many of the technologies explored here, those which benefit pupils with challenging behaviour will need to be tailored to the specific needs of individuals – e.g. 'Fledglings' produce a fact sheet about technology for pupils who bite or chew themselves, others or particular things. While all technological approaches will require the support of whole-school policies and staff commitment, those linked to supporting behaviour are particularly vulnerable if the approach chosen is not consistent throughout the learning environment.

Window on research

Biofeedback and anger management

It can be very challenging for teachers to support pupils who have emotional difficulties. This can include pupils who over-express, and those who under-express, emotion. Literature has emphasized the cognitive at the expense of the emotional and social dimensions of learning (Illeris, 2014). It may help you to deepen your understanding of emotion (e.g. Power and Dalgleigh, 2016) and to be aware that technology can sometimes help pupils with their emotions. For example, anger is a common human emotion, not always resulting in aggressive acts. Appropriate anger can be cathartic, and repressed anger can lead to violence. Furthermore, aggression does not always require anger (Henwood, Chou and Browne, 2015). Biofeedback can monitor and make use of a diverse range of physiological activities (e.g. breathing, skin temperature or brain waves) and has been applied to a range of different health conditions (Hillman and Chapman, 2018).

Bioresponsive games use information from sensors attached to the player to influence play. This has been developed into therapeutic tools to help pupils with emotional regulation difficulties like anger management problems. For example, 'Mightier' uses a heart rate monitor on the wrist of the player, and as the emotions of the player get stronger the game gets harder. The game guides the user to calm themselves as they play. The aim is transferability of anger management skills learned during the game into other situations or interactions. The intervention's efficacy was tested in a double-blind, randomized control trial (Kahn et al., 2013) with thirty-eight participants aged nine to seventeen, and it reported a statistically significant reduction in anger intensity for the treatment group. This study took place in an inpatient psychiatric unit, and the intervention lasted for one hour each day for five days.

Other studies support the possibility that biofeedback may be an effective tool for addressing anger management. Literature about biofeedback for anger management was reviewed by Hillman and Chapman (2018), who conclude that more research is necessary for this field with larger numbers of participants, using research designs that isolate the potential effects of biofeedback from the influences of other treatments, which test the effectiveness of such interventions in diverse settings, and which investigate how long-lasting these treatments may be.

Pupils sometimes referred to as 'gifted and talented' and people who have DME

Using technology to meet the needs of highly academically able or talented pupils was reviewed by Sprague and Shaklee (2015). However, some pupils identified as gifted and talented may also have special educational needs. These pupils may then be considered to have dual or multiple exceptionalities (DME). This means they have a SEN alongside a high learning potential (e.g. autism and artistic talent).

Just as it is important to ensure pupils with special educational needs can reach their potential, it is equally so for more able learners. Swan et al. (2015) explored how a school used a Virtual Learning Lab (VLL) and found, among other things, that it allows pupil control of the work pace which can then be increased when required. Also, QR codes on tablets or smartphones can connect pupils to differentiated activities

(Siegle, 2015) which allow pupils to easily access differentiated material. There are also coding platforms (occasionally free) available, providing a challenging learning environment (Siegle, 2017) where pupils can be encouraged and helped to go beyond the passive use of technology. Pupil-created video and pupil-led video analysis are stimulating for some, though barriers to video use as an instructional strategy should also be considered (Norton and Hathaway, 2010) and video should not be used as a substitute for direct engagement. Interactive Whiteboards could often be used more effectively by pupils (Northcote et al., 2010). Pupil-led data-logging in science lessons can be inspiring for some. For example, seeing a line graph being drawn in real-time of a substance freezing (like stearic acid) can help the understanding both of changes of state, and of what a line graph represents. This can connect some pupils to the world of professional science where such technology is ubiquitous. Virtual reality (VR) and augmented reality (AR) systems like Microsoft HoloLens 2, detecting the user's eye and hand movements, are used by some teachers (Billinghurst and Duenser, 2012). Where funding allows, a Tangible Interactive Tabletop could be worthwhile (Dillenbourg and Evans, 2011) as pupils can interact with each other while interacting with high-quality web-based resources (e.g. PhET simulations).

Reflective questions: A technology inventory

1. What technology do pupils in your class have access to at home and in school?
2. Are you confident teaching with the technology the pupils use? Consider how this influences your lesson planning and teaching.

What evidence is there of the impact of technology on learning of pupils with diverse learning needs?

Hattie (2009, pp. 221–32) synthesized seventy-six meta-analyses of 4,498 studies on computer-assisted instruction, and overall found a medium effect ($d = 0.37$). This means it is not obvious that computer-assisted instruction will raise attainment (but it is unlikely to lower it). He argues that you promote effective computer use if you:

- supplement rather than replace teaching
- train teachers sufficiently
- provide multiple learning opportunities
- allow pupils more control of their learning
- encourage peer learning (student/student and teacher/teacher)
- use feedback effectively.

The most effective aspect of computer-assisted instruction according to Hattie (2009) was when video technology was incorporated into lessons ($d = 0.52$).

Common interventions in school for gifted and talented pupils include ability grouping, enrichment (using activities to broaden the education of a group of pupils) and acceleration (moving through a curriculum faster or at an earlier age than usual). According to Hattie (2009), the most effective, and least used, of these is **acceleration** ($d = 0.84$), compared to an effect size of $d = 0.39$ for enrichment and $d = 0.30$ for ability grouping. Teachers can use technology to help more able pupils in a mixed-ability class:

> Technology, specifically Internet communication technologies, provides unique opportunities for gifted students so that acceleration and enrichment options can be made available.
>
> (Housand and Housand, 2012, p. 709)

Reflexive question: Research-inspired practice

How might your own experiences of using technology generally and in schools, and your knowledge of research evidence about technology and pupils with SEN/DME/gifted and talented, influence your classroom practice and understanding of pedagogy?

Barriers to successful assistive technology implementation

You are probably all already very aware of the following potential barriers. Think carefully as you read through these whether they have influenced your professional decisions and how you might overcome them in the future. First, resources and/or support services are sometimes unavailable for financial reasons. Second, users and/or educators may lack the necessary information about what resources are available, and how to use them effectively. Third, technology is sometimes unreliable. Fourth, support for users and their educators is sometimes sporadic. Fifth, users sometimes struggle to access a suitable needs-assessment before a device can be selected and also can have trouble getting their existing practice evaluated. Sixth, poorly designed or inappropriate devices can cause social problems for users. Finally, technology can be too complicated for the user and/or their educators to use or maintain. Modifications and updates to technology do not necessarily benefit users who have become proficient and familiar with a device or software, which then changes in ways which de-skills current users. The range of challenges in achieving competent use of assistive and inclusive technology for people with learning differences and the difficulties for those who support them should not be underestimated.

Reflective questions: Barriers

1. What barriers impede successful assistive technology implementation in your experience?
2. Which barriers can you and/or others do something about, and which are currently insurmountable?
3. What support do you have with technology in the classroom?
4. What support do you need?
5. How might you negotiate that support?

Classroom technology in the future

Teachers developing better pedagogy

The pedagogy associated with technology is termed 'technogogy' (Slough and Connell, 2006). Educational research into the effectiveness of technological interventions is useful background for teachers but is insufficient in itself. For example, an intervention without good support in research literature may nevertheless be the most appropriate one for a teacher to use in a particular context (especially if it facilitates an individual child to access learning in some way). What matters is that teachers, with the help of teacher educators, educational researchers and continuous professional development (CPD), develop wise pedagogical judgement (Biesta, 2015). How can you assess, review and enhance your use of assistive and inclusive technology?

Teachers considering using the SAMR model

SAMR stands for substitution, augmentation, modification and redefinition. You may find the **SAMR** model for technology integration (Hayhoe, 2015) useful for developing assistive and inclusive technologies in your school. The following example illustrates how the **SAMR** model can help when considering supporting pupils with visual impairment, including the academically highly able and/or those with additional special educational needs. Mylar paper is made from a material which 'bounces back' when pressure is applied, producing a raised image that is not reversed.

- Substituting technology involves simply encouraging pupils to use the technology as a replacement with no functional change – e.g. using embossed printing from a standard laser printer like Touchable Ink avoids the expense of a specialized embossing printer.

- **Augmentation** is where the technology mirrors the existing one but involves some functional improvement – e.g. a modern Braille Embosser printer, like the Juliet 120, prints to Braille directly from translation software (e.g. Duxbury DBT) and has a built-in translator. This translates and prints Word or pdf files directly. It also creates and edits tactile graphics.
- **Modification** of technology leads to a significant redesign of tasks – e.g. the BLITAB tactile tablet allows visually impaired users to extract tactile information from a tablet screen.
- Finally, **Redefinition** involves customized technology and the development of new tasks and associated skills. Future technology could be a tactile tablet where haptic information can be extracted from the screen, and also interaction with the embossed and debossed information could provide input to the computer. This future 'Interactive Tactile Tablet' would resemble an interactive 3D topographic map but be portable and is likely to be useful beyond the visually impaired. Potentially, using such a device as 3D interactive sculpture software (like Pixologic Sculptris) could be controlled with the hands with haptic feedback. Users could experience what the virtual 'clay' on the screen feels like as they mould it.

Thinking in this structured **SAMR** way offers all teachers the opportunity to step through the support being offered and consider the scale of the change the technology might bring. Technology should not be introduced into pedagogy without appropriate consideration of the changes to the pupil's skill and knowledge that will be required to ensure a successful implementation.

What do you conclude from this?

Technology is clearly important in the present and future lives of pupils

The ultimate aim of improving assistive technology use by pupils with diverse learning needs is to increase the pupils' inclusive technical capital (Hayhoe et al., 2015). Wherever possible, educators should welcome, adapt and embrace mainstream technology in the classroom to aid pupils' learning. It is your responsibility as a teacher to help pupils integrate inclusive and assistive technology into learning where this may help. Reflecting on technology use in the classroom can help you recognize your strengths and limitations. What technological knowledge and skills might need development or be lacking? How can you ensure your technological deficiencies do not hold pupils back in their engagement with technology? Teachers also have a safeguarding responsibility to help vulnerable pupils use technology safely (e.g. online privacy, sexting, online grooming, cyberbullying etc.), but its huge positive potential for pupils with diverse learning needs must not be underestimated.

It is best to design curricula from the start to be inclusive

Curricula, for all pupils, can and should be designed from the start to include assistive and inclusive technology (Mitchell, 2007). Universal Design for Learning (UDL) (Edyburn, Kavitha and Hariharan, 2017) acknowledges that pupils consist of diverse populations with different needs, experiences, understandings and approaches to learning. UDL is a process by which a curriculum (i.e. objectives, teaching methods, materials and assessments; Egan, 1978) is intentionally and systematically designed from the outset to reduce barriers, optimize levels of challenge and support individual differences.

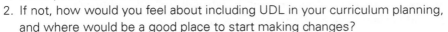

Reflective questions: UDL

1. Does your school's curriculum include UDL?
2. If not, how would you feel about including UDL in your curriculum planning, and where would be a good place to start making changes?

Next steps

The Student Environment Tasks Tools (SETT) (Zabala, 2005) is a framework that assists teams in supporting the decision-making process about assistive technology. This could be useful for school leadership teams. Teachers have a responsibility for ensuring assistive and inclusive technology is used effectively in their classroom. School leaders and policymakers have a responsibility in developing a school culture where teachers are supported in progressing this aspect of their practice, and guidelines might help (e.g. Wright et al., 2011).

Implications for educators

Some of the professional responsibilities of the teacher have been discussed throughout this chapter. The breadth and complexity of this topic do not permit a simple list of implications to be presented. Instead, we argue that teachers are best positioned to make judgements about technology, drawing on their own experience and that of others, in their complex social contexts. This is never straightforward but is already achieved by many school-based colleagues daily and is certainly being embraced by children and their families in the wider culture.

Annotated bibliography

Adam, T. and Tatnall, A. (2017). 'The value of using ICT in the education of school students with learning difficulties', *Education and Information Technologies*, 22(6), pp. 2711–26.
A useful text for educators using assistive technology with people who have **learning difficulties**.

Borg, J., Larsson, S. and Östergren, P. O. (2011). 'The right to assistive technology: For whom, for what, and by whom?', *Disability & Society*, 26(2), pp. 151–67.
Boser, K. I., Goodwin, M. S. and Wayland, S. C. (2014). *Technology tools for students with Autism: Innovations that enhance independence and learning*. Baltimore, MD: Brookes.
A review of technology designed for people with **Autism**.

Murchland, S. and Parkyn, H. (2010). 'Using assistive technology for schoolwork: The experience of children with physical disabilities', *Disability and Rehabilitation: Assistive Technology*, 5(6), pp. 438–47.
A useful further reading which explores the experiences of children with **physical differences** who use assistive technology.

Perelmutter, B., McGregor, K. K. and Gordon, K. R. (2017). 'Assistive technology interventions for adolescents and adults with learning disabilities: An evidence-based systematic review and meta-analysis', *Computers and Education*, 114, pp. 139–63.
A useful overview of research about assistive technology designed for people with **learning difficulties** which includes information about Speech, Language and Communication Difficulties.

Slovák, P. and Fitzpatrick, G. (2015). 'Teaching and developing social and emotional skills with technology', *ACM Transactions on Computer-Human Interaction (TOCHI)*, 22(4), p. 19.
Technology for people with **behavioural difficulties**.

Sprague, D. R. and Shaklee, B. (2015). 'Differentiating through technology for gifted students', in *Cases on instructional technology in gifted and talented education*. Hershey, PA: IGI Global, pp. 269–86.
Information about using technology to extend the learning of people sometimes called '**gifted and talented**'.

Tutt, R., Powell, S. and Thornton, M. (2006). 'Educational approaches in autism: What we know about what we do', *Educational Psychology in Practice*, 22(1), pp. 69–81.
United Nations (2007). *Convention on the rights of persons with disabilities*. Resolution 61/106. New York: United Nations.

6

Empowerment – The Power of Observation and Listening

Joy Mower and Teresa Dowling

Introduction

This chapter considers how teachers can empower pupils with additional needs, in mainstream and specialized settings, by listening to them and taking their voices into account. Listening can mean creating *explicit* opportunities for pupils to reflect on their perceptions of being a learner in a school which can inform professional decision-making and ongoing practice. It is also a key *implicit* aspect of good practice within the classroom. Understanding how individuals are experiencing the learning environment allows flexibility, and appropriate responses, in the moment. Willingness to hear children's voices also requires listening to those around them. Parents have 'funds of knowledge' (Moll et al., 1992) not just about their children as individuals, but about the socio-cultural contexts of their lives beyond school. This can help them to be their children's best advocates. 'Parents', throughout the chapter, will be used in the wider sense: encompassing all carers with parental responsibilities. Since your own individual thoughts and feelings influence your actions and interactions in the classroom, reflective and reflexive questions on key issues are provided throughout the chapter.

It is easier to hear the voices of others when we acknowledge our own, taking responsibility for it. Emotional responsibility requires awareness and self-awareness, of our own needs, and others'. Social responsibility requires respect for others; considering whose voices are listened to, and how to listen to voices which are more difficult to hear (or perceived as less valid or important). To effectively hear pupil's voices, teachers must consider *how* to listen – and develop skills in listening through observation, using their eyes *and* their ears. Awareness of pupil's thoughts and feelings does not imply that they have the knowledge and experience to make all decisions independently; rather, that decisions are informed by understanding pupil's experiences and the consequences of these. This chapter will consider whose voices need to be heard, why it is sometimes difficult to hear or interpret them, and how you can develop effective listening, in order to hear each pupil as an individual – as well as their advocates in order to empower them.

The chapter will cover:

- Listening to pupils: respecting all voices, empowering all pupils
- Pupil Voice in classroom practice: providing space for pupils to talk about their learning experience and empowering them to shape it
- Hearing through observation: pupils communicate through action as well as speech
- Listening to parents: effective approaches to communication and identifying barriers.

Listening to pupils: Respecting all voices, empowering all

Teachers are faced with a 'dilemma of difference' (Norwich, 2002), in which 'additionality' can cause tension with 'inclusivity'. Perceived differences can cause disadvantage and marginalization (Murdick et al., 2004) and defining pupils by their additional needs can be considered a form of 'othering'. Messiou (2019) observed teachers categorizing pupils within broad groupings, prompted by educational policy, for example, by grouping pupils who have 'Special Educational Needs' (SEN) and those that do not. This approach homogenizes pupils with SEN, ignoring the range and diversity of their needs. Teachers were also observed to categorize pupils by ability (Messiou, 2019). Pupils with high intellectual capacity are as prone to marginalization as any with additional needs, and teachers also express anxiety about meeting their social and academic needs (Geake and Gross, 2008).

Professionals' own personal emotional responses when working with pupils with additional needs also influence the decisions they make on behalf of the pupils (Marrable, 2014). Teachers often express idealism and determination to empower pupils by facilitating their right of expression, but the relationship and power balance between pupil and adult are always unequal and pupils' lives are governed by forces over which they have little say or control. Despite good intentions, a range of factors, including systemic and institutional practices, often mean that teachers' concerns about control in the classroom are prioritized over pupils' views or agency (Sergeant and Gillet-Swann, 2015). The result is twofold disempowerment, as the power balance in the classroom is firmly reinforced and pupils learn that their voices have little value.

To explore reflexively the degree to which you value the voices of pupils with additional needs, consider your attitudes to *all* pupils' voices, regardless of needs, status or diagnoses (https://www.un.org/development/desa/dspd/world-social-report/2020-2.html). This will enable you to consider the extent to which you enable pupils to express their needs, feelings and opinions – and be heard – as well as whether the way in which you listen *changes*, according to how you view the pupil and their capacity to express themselves. Listening to *any* pupil requires teachers to trust and respect their ability to communicate their feelings.

Reflective questions

1. Do you attach the same significance to the voices of *all* your pupils?
2. Do you respond to pupils in different ways, according to: their ability to communicate effectively; or your *perception* of their cognitive ability; or because of the relationship you have with them?

Reflexive question

Do you think your own personal experiences may have influenced your views or beliefs when thinking about pupil voice?

Pupil voice in classroom practice: Providing space for pupils to talk about and shape their learning experience

The new sociology of childhood rejects the socialization view of children as 'adults in the making' in favour of seeing them as autonomous beings, active in making sense of their worlds, and participating in them (James, Jenks and Prout, 1998), regardless of age or cognitive functioning. Pupils' learning experiences can be enriched when their right to participate in creating them is recognized by an adult; pupils are then empowered when this is realized in practice and leads to action. The UN Convention on the Rights of the Child (United Nations General Assembly, 1989) not only expects professionals to obtain their pupils' views but enshrines the right of children to express them however they choose. Central to the Convention on the Rights of Persons with Disabilities (United Nations General Assembly, 2006: Article 7) is that children with disabilities have equal rights to 'express their views freely on all matters affecting them ... the right to exercise control over the things which have a material impact on life, and to participate fully in society'. This recognizes that pupils with disabilities may need support in realizing that right and, therefore, that providing this support is an integral and inseparable part of that right.

When consulted about their education, pupils can offer insights to shape practice and policy (Prunty, Dupont and McDaid, 2012). Even very young pupils can form and express views; but their voices can be 'diluted' or 'filtered' (Wall et al., 2019) due to their inability to verbalize their thoughts. The same can be said for pupils with language difficulties, whether through delay in development or a disorder. The need to fit in can inhibit pupils further, including those considered high achievers, from expressing themselves, for fear of being different and standing out (Prior, 2011). Pupils with additional needs encompass those with disabilities and special gifted and talented and these two categories are not mutually exclusive, of course. Policy around 'Gifted and Talented' (GT) may vary across settings, jurisdictions and countries, and change over time, but the risk of marginalization is a constant and GT children's needs are emotional, as well as academic, which can be so easily overlooked.

Window on research

Messiou's (2012) research study – 'Collaborating with children in exploring marginalization: An approach to inclusive education' – is underpinned by the belief that pupils themselves can provide insights into the processes that both foster, and create barriers to, inclusion. The study recognized that to capture pupils' voices, a variety of both verbal and visual methods are needed. Through these the pupils were empowered as active participant researchers rather than passive objects of research. The tendency to consider inclusion only in relation to pupils with specific identified characteristics (e.g. special educational needs) who have, historically, been at great risk of marginalization is challenged. A concept of inclusion is suggested, that is not centred on the pupil and their individual characteristics, but uses Clark et al.'s (1999) 'organisational paradigm' that considers systems and structures.

By listening to the pupils, alternative perspectives were heard that demonstrated that practices that were designed and implemented in the classroom in order to support them could be experienced very differently by the pupils themselves. The practice of grouping pupils according to attainment in a subject was one example. Organizing pupils into different classes or groups within the class so that they are working with pupils whose current understanding and targets are similar is often considered to be a supportive practice that meets their needs. Pupils in lower attaining groups, however, were unhappy as they felt they missed the opportunity to work with their higher-achieving peers, which they felt would be beneficial. Embarrassment was also expressed by pupils at being labelled as lower ability, and others knowing.

Pupils' thoughts on the choice of work on display around the school also demonstrated a disparity between teachers' efforts to develop an inclusive classroom that celebrated pupils' achievements, and pupils understanding about the criteria for choosing work to display; this led to feelings of marginalization. Teachers believed that they were choosing work that had shown effort as well as success, but the pupils were either unaware of this, or did not feel it matched their actual experience. Providing pupils with an opportunity to share their thoughts also created a space in which they were able to collaborate in finding solutions; in this case the pupils suggested keeping a record of whose work had been displayed to ensure fairness and the valuing of all their work.

School councils can provide an empowering forum for pupils to articulate, share and discuss their perspectives on all aspects of their school lives. However, their effectiveness depends on the views of the adults involved: whether they see them as fulfilling a policy demand or have a genuine commitment to the agency of the pupils (Fielding, 2001). The tokenistic view can have a greater negative impact on pupils than if no such forum existed (Alderson, 2000). This reinforces the fact that pupils often have little choice over what they are being asked to give opinions on, the ways they are allowed to express them, or both (Hart, 1992; Lundy, 2018). Avoiding tokenism requires analysis of the questions' pupils are asked, as well as the situations and physical, temporal, social and emotional spaces in which they are asked to contribute.

Many school councils mimic adult committees, with a heavy reliance on traditional literacies. The attributes of a good school councillor are considered as 'strong communication skills and organisation', which can exclude many pupils. To develop greater potential for participation, methods developed for participative research with pupils can be utilized in classrooms and across schools, enabling them to express their views, via a range of communicative models including drawing, collage, drama and photography, as in Messiou's (2012) research. Cox and Robinson Pant (2006) found that in school councils where non-verbal communication was included (in this case, mapping, drawing, card-ranking and timelines) participation increased and it led to a change in understanding of the concept of participation, for both adults and pupils.

For further examples of methods to consider in your classroom or school, see Clark and Moss's (2011) 'Mosaic approach', for listening to young children, which can be adapted for additional needs, and the creative methodologies of Long et al. (2012) to elicit the views of young learners with additional needs in literacy.

Reflective questions

1. Are there spaces within your classroom (temporal and spatial) which could be developed to enable pupil collaborative participation in decision-making?
2. Which methods could you use to enable participation of all pupils?

Hearing through observation: Pupils communicate through action as well as speech

Providing explicit opportunities for pupils to speak and be heard can address *some* organizational issues which disempower them, but this is not enough. Individual voices also need to be heard, within the day-to-day interactions of the classroom, for teachers to be aware of, and respond to, immediate concerns.

A teacher's intention may be to give pupils a voice, but they may be inefficient at communicating their needs and unable to verbalize their communication, especially if anxious, hurt or worried. This can be exacerbated for those pupils whose additional needs are directly or indirectly related to speech, language and/or communication difficulties. As with any interaction, the 'language' needs to be understood. There can also be a further struggle to communicate in situations where pupils are overwhelmed and their ability to self-regulate may be compromised. Additionally, some forms of communication are challenging for teachers to experience and can feel deliberately provocative especially when a teacher is trying to meet expectations of maintaining control of themselves and others. Teachers must also develop the habit of listening through focused observation to recognize each pupil's behaviours and what they 'say'.

The case study below highlights the importance of listening through observation. An example of what the teacher might have considered a 'critical incident' (Brookfield, 1990) is examined; it emphasizes the interplay between 'long-term' and 'in-the-moment' listening, and demonstrates how understanding a pupil's concerns in a *particular* situation requires an understanding of the pupil, drawn from observation, not just at the specific time, but across a wide range of circumstances. In this case study the pupil involved has an autistic spectrum disorder (ASD) which results in high anxiety, often exhibited as challenging behaviour.

Case study: Integration of pupil with autistic spectrum disorder (ASD) into a mainstream classroom for mathematics lessons

Country: UK

Age group: Year 4

Setting: Max attended a Specialist Resource Provision (SRP) for pupils with a primary need of ASD. He was an able child, but, due to his ASD, he found the sensory challenges of a mainstream school challenging. An SRP supports pupils in continuing to access mainstream education; staff were working with Max to enable his integration into a subject he found motivating – maths.

Participants involved: Max; Special Educational Needs Co-ordinator (SENCO); Teaching Assistant (TA); Teacher. Names have been changed, but the case represented is a snapshot of actual events which occurred in Max's integration experience.

Case study

Prior to any integration, the SENCO and supporting adult worked with him to create a social story about his partner class and created a map so he knew how to get from the SRP building to his mainstream classroom and back again. They also worked to create a low-stimuli, individual workstation within the partner classroom. Max began to visit the classroom when it was empty, except for the teacher, completing maths work, and beginning to build a relationship with the teacher.

When Max appeared content with the routine, and cognitively able to access the mathematics, the SENCO gradually increased the number of pupils in the room. Max continued to cope well and began joining his partner class during the final ten minutes of each maths lesson. This back-chaining was very successful and was increased incrementally until Max could successfully integrate for the whole lesson, with support.

One day, Max arrived in the classroom and the teacher had not changed the Interactive Whiteboard slide from English to maths. Max stayed and sat down but started to growl. The teacher explained that she would change the board in one minute, when everyone had finished. After precisely one minute, the teacher did not change the slide; Max tipped over a table and ripped up his maths book. He then swore, before running out of class. The teacher felt that his behaviour was too challenging to have back in her class.

Outcomes

In the situation described, the teacher had tried to listen, and communication had been, initially, successful. Integration had been taken at Max's speed and appropriate supports had been put in place. However, when the classroom situation meant that the teacher minimized or misunderstood Max's increasing anxiety, it escalated to the point that he could no longer self-regulate, despite his attempts to communicate his need for the teacher to move the whiteboard display onto maths content. He even accepted a one-minute wait. However, when this was not followed through, he was unable to contain his anxiety. The teacher saw this as challenging or inappropriate behaviour, rather than hearing it as an expression of heightened anxiety and inability to cope. The situation became about control, rather than communication. Max's anxiety caused a panic attack, but the teacher was also experiencing feelings about loss of control and fears for safety within the classroom.

Max felt anxious, stressed and unsafe because:	If the teacher observed and listened to Max, both regularly and 'in the moment', she might have reduced his anxiety by:
He was in a mainstream class of thirty pupils	Issuing him with an 'exit card' to use when feeling anxious or overwhelmed, in order to leave the classroom in a controlled way
His perception that he had arrived in an English, not a maths, lesson	Warning him that the lesson had overrun and maths would start late
He had unexpected unstructured time while the rest of the class finished their English	Providing him with a 'Maths Pack' with independent activities, for any unstructured time
His understanding of 'wait a minute' literally; he expected the teacher to change to maths in exactly sixty seconds	Understanding the way that Max hears and responds to idioms and figures of speech and adjusting her language

What we can learn

The freeze, fight or flight sensation is the body's natural response to danger. In pupils with high levels of anxiety, such as Max, this response is triggered easily. In situations such as this, anxiety is likely to be compounded where a pupil is less able to interpret and rationalize the actions of others effectively, due to poor or under-developed theory of mind (Astington and Edward, 2010; Baron-Cohen, Tager-Flusberg and Cohen, 1994). Max's initial response appeared to be fight; first, by tipping the table and ripping his work; followed by flight, when he left the classroom. Either way, he was communicating to the teacher that he no longer felt safe. When pupils feel these sensations, it is important that the teacher does not interpret this as a planned or deliberate provocation. The teacher and TA could have listened to Max's initial communication that he was becoming anxious. Growling was the first sign that his anxiety was increasing and, at this point, de-escalation strategies could have been attempted.

The case study shows the importance of observation when listening. Had the teacher been watching Max, she would have seen, as well as heard, signs of his growing anxiety; but she had many other things to attend to at the same time. How could the situation have been handled differently? Could competing priorities have been managed differently, for a more successful outcome? The central issue was the tension between Max's needs and the teacher's responsibility to ensure the majority of the class finished their previous task. Had Max hyperventilated, rather than tipping the table, would the teacher have responded differently, with sympathy, rather than annoyance? Did she consider what her own responses communicated, in return?

A safe learning environment is fundamental to all pupils' ability to achieve (Maslow, 1954) and a part of a teacher's emotional responsibility to provide for them. Nurturing safety requires understanding of what is being communicated by different behaviours, including your own, and other adults, as well as the pupils; considering what a pupil is communicating before responding. When juggling practical and logistical aspects of classroom management, alongside a focus on learning goals for other pupils, it takes practice to be continually listening and responding to the emotional needs of all the class. There were a number of points in the case study where, had the teacher understood what Max was trying to communicate, the outcome could have been different. It is also worth considering damage done to the pupil/teacher relationship if the miscommunication is perceived, unfairly, to be the fault of the pupil – and what steps could be taken to repair this. For example, after the event, the teacher could also have demonstrated that she was listening by creating a Social Story to empower Max with strategies to use, should the situation recur.

It can be difficult to hear what a pupil is saying when their means of communication does not conform to what you as a teacher are accustomed to or find acceptable. Strategies for addressing this include opportunities for continuing professional development, focusing on the general *and* specific. Teachers need to understand communication difficulties which pupils with different needs may experience, as well as having a thorough knowledge of the individual needs and behaviours of every pupil they teach. The responsibility for supporting teachers in this lies partly within schools' staff development processes, but there may also be deep-rooted attitudes and assumptions which need to be explored, to allow teachers to be able to observe, as well as listen to, the voice of every one of their pupils.

Reflective questions

1. What have you observed that demonstrates a pupil is expressing a feeling or thought through their actions, even if they cannot articulate it in words?
2. What responses have the pupils learned to expect from you? Do these responses affect what they say, or the ways in which they say it?

Reflexive questions

1. How good are you at ensuring pupils with additional needs are even heard (and especially) when their means of communication is a challenge to your own beliefs about appropriate classroom behaviour?
2. Why do you think you respond in this way?

Listening to parents: Effective approaches to communication and identifying barriers

Legislation in many English-speaking countries (such as the Special Educational Needs and Disabilities 0–25 code of practice (DfE and DoH, 2014, 2015) in England) has moved towards ensuring parents have a greater say in their child's education and healthcare. This has placed a greater legal – as well as moral – obligation on professionals to work in partnership and to empower parents, as advocates for their children. In focusing on pupils with additional needs and considering difference and diversity, it is also important to recognize commonality. Ferguson and Asche (1989, p. 108) noted that the most important thing about a pupil with disabilities is that they are a child; and that the most important thing about the parents of a child with disabilities is that they are, first and foremost, parents. At the heart of the matter is the understanding that the general concerns of parents are the same regardless of whether their child has special educational needs, disabilities or gifts and talents.

Where provision for pupils with specific needs may require the specialist knowledge and support of a number of professionals, the voices of their parents can become marginalized and this can cause conflict and tension. Despite research which suggests there is a positive impact when parents are involved in their children's education, parents can be seen by professionals as detrimental to the well-being and development of their children. For children with disabilities, a 'deficit approach', where a pupil is identified with their disability, can have a considerable impact on the way they are listened to, and the way in which those around them interact, with them, and each other. If a pupil is identified by a 'label', those with specialist knowledge may perceive themselves and/or be perceived by others as 'the experts'; the deficit perception is sometimes extended to the whole family (Turnbull and Turnbull, 2002) and the result may be that the parent and pupil views may not be valued. Parents of gifted and talented pupils may not feel confident about their own knowledge of how best to support them and may also experience hostility within the community towards their child (Koshy, Smith and Brown, 2017). Where a pupil is seen as an individual, the experts are those who know the child best – the child and parents – and then the professionals who work with the family.

Window on research

In 'Until somebody hears me: Parent voice and advocacy in special educational decision making', Hess, Molina and Kozleski (2006) considered the difficulties parents may face as they encounter 'the world of special education' (ibid.) and negotiate a path within this. The study was situated in the United States where the writers had experience as a school psychologist, a bilingual counsellor and a special education teacher. They explored how educational professionals can build relationships which are supportive, but also respect parents as equal partners. The study identified three themes which all present tensions between competing needs and agendas, for parents, teachers and within schools as institutions. These tensions are not all between stakeholders, but also for stakeholders. Parents may opt for 'passive compliance' (ibid., p. 151) where advocacy may risk creating conflict with professionals who are perceived as more expert and more powerful. Teachers may find that their role as 'the experts' conflicts with their role as family-support. The data suggest that the processes in schools which are set up to be effective and efficient on the wider scale may fail to provide for specific needs at an individual level.

The study also identifies trust and communication as central to equal partnerships between parents and professionals in special educational contexts. Additionally, family cultures may be poorly understood by professionals, and where inaction is rooted in a lack of trust, it may be mistakenly perceived as a lack of interest or cooperation. Methods of communication (e.g. letters and forms) considered normal within a professional culture may alienate parents for whom these are overly formal and unfamiliar ways of sharing information. Low levels of education and lack of proficiency in the dominant language may compound this. Systems, which appear to include parents, may be in place but being invited to be present at a meeting is not the same as feeling able to speak up or believing that you will be heard.

A teacher's relationship with a pupil was cited in the data as the factor that was most important to parents. The interpersonal aspect of the relationship was more significant than the experience and qualifications of the teacher. Where support for education, social care and health is outlined in an individual plan, parents expect to see this acted on. The study reports an instance of a pupil with a hearing impairment where the teacher consistently did not wear the amplification device; excuses were made about it being broken, but no action was taken. If parents perceive a lack of engagement from the teacher, trust is not maintained. Parents want a teacher who cares about their child, spends time getting to know their child, and treats them as an individual with emotional as well as academic needs.

One of the issues raised in Hess, Molina and Kozleski's (2006) research was concerned with parents' passive compliance. Parents may opt for passive compliance because they feel they do not have the power to advocate for their child. The power imbalance between parents and professionals affects the way that each respond to each other and prevents voices from being heard or even able to speak up; it is *disempowering*. Power imbalances are created, where there are 'insiders' – usually professionals – who know and understand the norms and language, and can operate with ease within a particular group or culture; and 'outsiders', for whom this lack of knowing is further disempowering, and who can view the 'insiders' as an impenetrable clique. This is very much the case in the field of Special Education, as in specialist areas of any kind, where there is jargon and a multitude of processes, often referred to by acronyms, and other unfamiliar terminology.

The power balance between teachers and parents can be qualitatively as well as quantitatively different, expressing itself in different ways, according to parents' own experiences, capabilities and needs. Even where parents have the cultural capital (Bourdieu, 1986) such as the educational skills and resilience to enable them to navigate through the forms, appointments and meetings, as is often necessary where children have additional needs, they may still feel like outsiders when they advocate for their children. This also means being aware of the perceptions of others about the role of the teacher and the status of professionals and how this might affect communication. The ways in which information is recorded and shared have many implications, too, and reflecting on this can also highlight attitudes to the value that is put on the information itself.

Listening to parents means recognizing different communication needs and the ways in which good communication can empower but poor communication disempowers. One response to parents asking for better communication is to send, for example, more emails, or newsletters, rather than to think about the form of the communication. Many of the methods used by schools rely on understanding and competency with particular forms of literacy; it may require parents to sift through text and pull out key information directly relevant to their child. This can be overwhelming for some parents and although the school feels that it has communicated thoroughly and efficiently, the parent may find it difficult to comprehend the information and feel frustrated and isolated.

Parents feel more able to respond when communication is in a familiar and comfortable medium. Increasingly, schools are using digital communication practices, but these can be merely informative or can enable interaction (Vigo-Arrazola and Dieste-Gracia, 2019). Websites tend to follow more traditional, one-directional forms of print communication. They are public spaces where access is open to all and not limited by membership, but they generally offer only information, rather than participation. Adopting text-messaging services, emails and apps which generate reports related to the school reward systems, such as Class Do Jo (https://www.classdojo.com/) or Carrot Rewards (https://www.carrotrewards.co.uk/), can help as the form of communication is familiar, immediate and informal. Social media, such as Facebook, can be used to create a 'dynamic, online social community' (ibid.) where being a parent is the criteria for membership of a group specifically aimed at developing and maintaining relationships between parents and school. Interaction is encouraged and provides opportunities for teachers and other professionals within the school to listen and respond to the interests, ideas and needs of members through their posting of messages, comments and 'likes'.

Reflective question

Are your communication methods focused on information sharing, or encouraging feedback?

Reflexive question

How do your own values and assumptions about different means and modes of communication (e.g. the method and language used) affect your ability to hear what is being said?

Implications for practice

Teachers must listen to, and hear, the views of *all* pupils, their caregivers and external professionals in order to develop children's ability to respond to the world as agentic and empowered individuals. The principles represented in children's rights under the UNCRC have been characterized by the three 'P's: Provision, Protection and Participation' (Hammarberg, 1990). Empowerment starts with participation and provision must honour and accept this participation, adapting to meet the needs of the pupil. Meeting the needs of all pupils and all the responsibilities of classroom teaching is a complex endeavour, but where pupil voices are listened to, situations in which they feel helpless or passive reduce, and motivation, engagement and self-esteem improve. To achieve this requires thoughtful consideration of how classroom routines and environments can be organized as places both where pupils feel safe and confident to speak and be heard, and where individual skills of observation and listening can be nurtured and developed. Pupils can then feel protected, respected and valued as active participants, empowered by their experience of education.

Annotated bibliography

Marrable, T. (2014). 'Emotion in responses to the child with "additional needs"',
    Child & Family Social Work, 19(4), pp. 401–10.
This paper considers the ways in which interactions between health, education and
social care practitioners and the children and parents they serve are emotion-laden,
and the effect of this on outcomes. A case study is used throughout, with extracts
demonstrating a range of perspectives which create a narrative that is both accessible
and relatable. It is an article that provokes self-reflection on our own personal/
professional interactions and how to acknowledge and manage our own emotions in
order to support children more effectively.

Norwich, B. (2002). 'Education, inclusion and individual differences: Recognising
    and resolving dilemmas', *British Journal of Educational Studies*, 50(4),
    pp. 482–502.
Brahm Norwich is a Professor of Educational Psychology and Special Educational
Needs and has researched extensively within these areas, including the experience of
special educational needs from the perspectives of children, parents and teachers. He
highlights a central tension that is present in the debate around special education and
inclusion within mainstream schools, asking whether if even referring to children's
needs as additional could be a form of discrimination in itself. He suggests that
different values need to be brought to bear so that personal and social learning are
also considered of worth when pursuing high standards of attainment for all.

Prunty, A., Dupont, M. and McDaid, R. (2012). 'Voices of students with special
    educational needs (SEN): Views on schooling', *Support for Learning*, 27(1),
    pp. 29–36.
The basis of inclusive practice must ensure that all pupils have a voice within their own
education and decisions that affect them, and although policy and legislation support
this, the degree to which it is understood and implemented varies. A methodology
that uses a range of methods is important when gathering the views of children with
a range of needs, but the underlying assumption must be that they have something to
say and have a right to be heard.

7

Working Together

Christian Couper and Sue Soan

Introduction

> *E hara taku toa i te toa takitahi, he toa takitini.*
> *(My strength is not as an individual, but as a collective)*

This chapter will provide you the expert, the teacher, with knowledge and practice examples of what 'working together' really means to enable positive outcomes to be achieved for pupils and their families. The first part of the chapter will provide a rationale for why working together can be considered positive for twenty-first-century education in schools for all pupils. We then move on to explore the benefits of teacher team working and collaboration in schools from the perspective of practitioners in New Zealand. The second part of the chapter will then explain why all teachers also need to be able to work with professionals from other disciplines. This is especially vital when working with pupils with a learning difference needing input from a range of professionals. Questions such as 'So what is it that enables a teaching team to work together effectively?' and 'How can this collaboration stretch to encompass and value professionals from other fields such as health, policing and social care?' will be answered. Forming productive relationships with professionals from other disciplines is not as straightforward as you might assume and so we will offer you ways to successfully establish and maintain these, sometimes, complex partnerships. We will also illustrate the difference these collaborations or partnerships can have on outcomes for pupils with additional needs.

Working together to meet the needs of pupils with diverse learning needs

Pupils are entering regular schooling with ever-increasing complex educational, health and social needs (further detail is provided in Chapter 3) and as such teachers need to be able to work with and integrate knowledge and skills from other professional disciplines in order to help the pupils engage successfully with learning. There is also a need to deliver a modern education system that is fit for purpose in a world that is rapidly changing, where pupils need competencies alongside knowledge to enable them to achieve a fulfilled and positive future. Due perhaps in response to these and other issues such as economic and employment pressures, natural disasters and practice development (e.g. inclusive practice and special educational needs), collaborative team working, integrated services and joint commissioning have been expanding across countries since the 1990s, with increasing speed. It is therefore vital that every teacher thinks about their role and personal, social and emotional responsibilities to initiate, maintain and develop professional relationships and not assume this can be left to school leaders such as Special Educational Needs Coordinators (SENCOs) or Principals in schools to manage. Without doubt this is a vital and complex skill which all teachers need to understand, and this is especially important when working with pupils with either special educational needs, gifts, and talents or both.

Therefore, as you read this chapter hold in mind the following reflective and reflexive statements and think about what, why and how you can develop your own skills in order to be able to confidently fulfil your teaching role and responsibilities when working together with others.

Reflective and reflexive questions

As a teacher what do you personally, socially and emotionally need to consider in order to enhance your skills when working in collaboration for the pupils with additional needs?

We consider this will include:

1. Acknowledge and feel comfortable with your ability to engage with and maintain professional responsibilities. It is vital that you can take personal responsibility to acknowledge the different requirements and boundaries between professions and their roles and responsibilities.
2. What are real and what are false boundaries? Ensure you understand the law(s) which you need to follow. Be aware of and accept limitations and accept support and leadership from a professional from another discipline. Take advice from others with different perspectives and develop a 360-degree perspective.
3. Demonstrate an ability to be genuine, be able to compromise, be flexible and be understanding. To be able to generate professional trust and reassure others by being reliable and trustworthy.

Reflective questions

1. Think carefully about how you establish and maintain professional relationships. What 'qualities' and skills do you use to make these positive and successful? Make a short list of these qualities and as you read through this chapter note how you can develop them further and why they might help you enhance your practice with pupils with special educational needs (SEN) or those with high academic or creative ability or both.

2. Be honest with yourself and write down (if you have) how you sometimes speak or think about other professionals, especially if they work within a different discipline. If you have not experienced this, can you remember a time when you have heard others speak of barriers to effective joint working?

Why work together?

To answer the question 'why work together?' it is helpful to revisit what we suggest is a generally accepted reason, for societies across the world, for maintaining teaching and learning within a school education system.

First, it needs to be acknowledged that the concept of collaboration, of working together, is not new to humanity. It is frequently said that when people work together a task that seems large for one can become a lot more manageable for the many. In England, the saying 'Many hands make light work', translated from 'Abema hamoi basindika eitara' (Haya Tanzania[1]), is a familiar phrase spoken to children by parents and teachers. Indeed, the fundamental security of efforts made in groups that reap greater outcomes for all spans many cultures in a similar form to describe the team approach to work. Succinctly, these sayings promote the idea that through working together people (adults and children) can, if they have the vision, achieve a greater outcome than they could achieve alone. So how does this way of thinking fit within a twenty-first-century education system for pupils with additional needs?

What is the purpose of working together in an inclusive education system: Aiming to include all pupils, whatever their learning differences?

Some theories posit that learning is a naturally social act (e.g. Rousseau, Mager) (Bailey et al., 2013; Gray and Macblain, 2012) and their creators believed that the

---

[1] https://www.afriprov.org/african-proverb-of-the-month/27-2001proverbs/171-oct2001.html

individual pupil should be educated for the benefit of wider societal good as well as themselves. Rousseau, who died just a decade before the start of the French Revolution (in 1778), saw it was the role of the tutor (teacher) to help shape the learning environment in which pupils would 'increase their understanding of such essential as humility, honesty and dishonesty, and respect for themselves and for others' (Gray and Macblain, 2012, p. 15), despite the fact that he thought society would ultimately corrupt them. Thus, the social and working together for the 'greater good' purpose of education has been a long-established approach in education, and we would argue is a core value held by the majority of teachers in practice to this day. But, how well do teachers model this collaborative, wider good approach to their daily teaching practice, when planning lessons or considering specific interventions or strategies for pupils with specific needs? In England, for example, all teachers are asked to provide SEN support and provision using an 'assess, plan, do and review' approach (DfE and DoH, 2014, 2015, p. 100) for pupils of all ages with special educational needs, within which different and additional support and intervention from other professionals (i.e. Occupational Therapists (OT), Speech and Language Therapists (SALT) and Educational Psychologists (EP)) should be woven seamlessly into their support plans or provision maps (Massey, 2016). Although not regarded in England as standard practice we would also recommend that it is good practice to ensure that the pupils with high ability or with dual or multiple exceptionalities (DME) also are included within this consistent, ongoing process of support and review.

Reflective question

How do you fulfil the statutory requirements of your country's legislation and statutory guidance with regards to providing learning that is inclusive of the needs of those pupils who require specific interventions or strategies from other colleagues or professionals?

A new way of working – an inclusive approach

There are many who now believe that to best prepare pupils to be successful in the future, teachers need to embrace diversity and focus on collaborative ways for teaching, and importantly practice collaborative ways for learning.

In New Zealand, collaborative teaching is already taking place as schools throughout New Zealand change their practice to meet the demands of this new century. As a consequence of the earthquakes of 2010 and 2011 in Christchurch (the largest city on New Zealand's South Island, *Te Waipounamu*), the school network was seriously damaged. Most schools had some repair work that was required before they could reopen and in response the Christchurch Schools Renewal programme[2]

---

[2]   https://www.education.govt.nz/our-work/changes-in-education/christchurch-schools-rebuild-programme-2013-2022/

was initiated through the Ministry of Education to repair, renew and rebuild schools. At the same time teachers were engaging with the Curriculum[3] which promoted the move for them to continually improve their work through inquiry. As a consequence of this, teachers began to collaborate in sharing their ways of working, their programme objectives and making use of the wisdom of others to overcome barriers. With the Renewal programme and the changing pedagogy there was the opportunity to align property design with teacher practice, and spaces were designed not around classroom size but around the teaching and learning.

What is collaborative learning in schools in New Zealand?

"He rangi tā matawhāiti, he rangi tā matawhānui."

> *(A person with narrow vision has a restricted horizon; a person with wide vision has plentiful opportunities.)*

Collaborative learning

It is important to understand the principles of collaborative learning and how a collaborative teaching team works before moving on to look at the case study example.

Table 7.1 describes collaborative learning in New Zealand in comparison to cooperative learning, giving a good idea of how the teaching and learning environment is constructed.

Table 7.1 Collaborative learning is not the same as Cooperative learning[1]

	Collaborative learning	Cooperative learning
1.	Collaborative tasks are group structured.	Cooperative learning activities are teacher structured.
2.	Pupils source what they need in collaborative tasks.	Material is teacher-supplied with cooperative learning.
3.	In collaborative work the success is assessed by individual and group assessment.	Success is defined by a teacher marking the finished project in cooperative work
4.	In collaborative work the teacher is another resource able to be accessed when the group needs.	In cooperative work the teacher monitors and intervenes when necessary.
5.	With collaborative learning the teacher doesn't have control over the end product or the direction the group decides to take in order to pursue what they see as a successful goal. This is more creative and can grow new skills for individuals, groupings and present unexpected outcomes.	With cooperative learning the teacher has a fair idea what the task is and where it will end up and the output expected.

[1] https://resourced.prometheanworld.com/collaborative-cooperative-learning/

[3] http://nzcurriculum.tki.org.nz/The-New-Zealand-Curriculum (page 30)

Collaborative teaching team

A collaborative teaching team is focused on each pupil's next step needs and how they as educators can take them to and through that next step. This team does not expect to be able to fulfil all of the pupils' needs, and unlike past models of one teacher–one class or grouping of pupils, provision of a quality and effective programme is designed to be well supported by collaboration of the teachers' technical strengths, experience and creative ideas. Most of all a collaborative teaching team will have committed to prepare together, expects to make mistakes, and has the will to find ways forward – together, by employing the talents and experience of the team.

For pupils and groups of pupils a collaborative teaching team can provide a learning programme with greater tailoring to meet individual pupil's needs, such as those who have specific talents or ability or those requiring special educational needs. These teams can also provide a faster response to changes across the holistic spectrum of education.

Considering this way of working from a parent and family perspective it can create more options for the formation of strong relationships, of mutual understanding about their child's well-being.

Reflexive questions

1. Whether you are a new teacher or experienced, how do you feel you would cope with teaching in a collaborative team?
2. Do you have any personal concerns that would hold you back from working in this way and why?
3. How would you cope with having no personal space of your own in school?

Reflective questions

1. Consider your current way of working in your school. What skills and qualities do you think you and other teachers would/do need to be an effective and efficient collaborative teaching team member?
2. How effective do you think this way of teaching is for pupils with special educational needs or those who have high ability, or both?

A collaborative teaching team

The following case study clearly identifies how collaboration can be seen as a really positive way of ensuring that every individual pupil in a class is taught and supported in order for them to feel successful and happy members of the community. However, the case study illustrates that it is not easy and does require a holistic approach from initial training to ongoing continuing professional and school development. The case study clearly identifies skills and qualities that teachers need for collaborative teaching to be successful.

Case study: A collaborative teaching team

Country: New Zealand

Age group: Years 3 and 4 (8–9-year-old primary school pupils)

Setting: Urban Primary School – Christchurch – New Zealand

Participants involved: One teacher, collaborating for the past 5 years with another.

The case study

How a teacher with more than 25 years in the classroom and experience at all levels of the primary education system made the adjustment to work collaboratively.

The teacher's story

Eddie[4] is an experienced teacher working in a small urban school in Christchurch, New Zealand. Eddie has 25 years of teaching experience across all levels of primary education and has had roles from classroom teacher through to senior management positions. Eddie retrained as a teacher, making the change from engineering to education. Eddie discovered that he was more of a people person and liked helping and working with children to find their success and improve their abilities. Eddie's current school is classified as lower socioeconomic, and Eddie enjoys seeing measured holistic improvements in the progress of pupil's he and his partner are responsible for.

Eddie is currently in a collaborative teaching position with nearly 60 children aged 8–9 years old with a partner teacher, unchanged since the school moved towards models of collaborative practice in 2015.

Eddie's school was one of many that was redeveloped following the earthquakes across Canterbury. Much of the previous school design was renewed over the existing footprint of the buildings to support flexible teaching and learning and to promote collaborative practice amongst staff.

---

[4] Not his real name.

Eddie says the largest space in their school could take up to three standard classes, approximately 90 pupils. Their design was based on a collaborative theory of the era, but he admits many of the spaces are not being used as initially designed. The practice of collaboration between teachers, pupils and support staff continues to drive an evolving approach to working together. Collaborative teams across the school each have a degree of autonomy to create their best collaborative approach and freedoms provided by their school principal seem to enable this ongoing development of professional practice.

Along with a change to collaborative practice, Eddie has adopted a pedagogy that aims to respond to the individualized learning needs of pupils. He and his partner teacher aim to carefully identify learner styles and tailor a classroom structure and plan that best fits their learning priorities. Eddie acknowledges that this approach can be challenging and often creates plenty of professional discussion about what is best.

Eddie has noticed that the biggest factors for success across school teams has been trusting relationships within teaching teams. He describes this as; the ability to listen and understand each other, the security in their relationship to say 'no' to something.

Eddie referred to his collaborative teaching relationship as 'a little like a marriage.' The building of an effective relationship to work together is a key element in a successful team. An important fact for new teachers to consider and for experienced teachers joining a collaborative team.

One example Eddie provided was the comment his partner said: 'I know now, to not come to you in the morning with a bright idea. That's not how you like to do things.' When collaborative partnerships work best, they make deliberate decisions about when and how they contribute their ideas to the collaborative partnership. Protocols for effective communication need to be found and tested as fit for purpose and that they fit the relationship.

Eddie thought that he and his partner have learnt they can't always challenge each other's ideas. They make shared choices about what and when their professional opinions are discussed, and fully appreciate they are unique professionals within a collaborative teaching relationship and are committed to working together for their pupils. Keeping the fundamental purpose of their collaboration at the front of things has enabled them to keep the positive developments of their practice moving in a direction they're happy with.

How things work in a collaborative teaching team

The teaching and learning programme is designed by them, for the needs of their pupils and to deliver within the school's broader routines. During the mornings learning groups are shared and the afternoon has more structure about what learning happens, for who and when. Individual children are shared, and each child's progress tracked.

A contributing factor to their collaborative success has been sharing an office space. The day is unpacked, their children discussed, knowledge is shared, and their teaching actions and decisions worked through. A high level of professional trust exists and is a key element to ongoing development and success of their collaborative relationship.

A significant focus for them is well-being of each other, and their pupils and colleagues (also see Chapter 3). They have developed an equitable flexibility within their relationship that allows for breaks, or changes to their programme to support necessary life happenings.

In the context of behaviour support, they find that their collaborative relationship can have a positive impact on how they care for their pupils. Each pupil has more than one teacher who supports them, both of their opinions become the foundation to interventions and the options are magnified when two teachers are involved.

In the case of one collaborative partner leaving the team, the relationship building process and operation would have to be renewed. A new teacher entering a collaborative team would need to join the team with full understanding of what is expected and what is open for change. A collaborative team seeking to fill a vacant position is just as vulnerable, in that they cannot stay as they were, they will also be required to change and most of all, both parties will need to put their pupils' needs first and quickly form high trust, professional relationships for teaching and learning.

Outcomes

1. The purpose for collaboration and the relationship between teachers are great contributors towards the success of this approach to teaching and learning.
2. Success of the approach should be measured holistically, and as an evolutionary.

What we can learn

1. Collaborate for a purpose.
2. Work on the relationships that enable pupils and teachers to be successful in their goals. Measure success holistically and never lose your focus on what is best for the pupil.
3. To prepare teachers for the demands of a collaborative role, certain skills need to be prioritized in teacher training. These are clearly detailed in Figure 7.1 but also include:

i) Specific interpersonal skills that facilitate adults to work closely and respectfully together. Listening skills and developing the ability to ask questions or challenge opinions in a relationship-enhancing way.

ii) Team building and being genuine are important considerations. Specific training in how to express opinions, resolve conflicts and make difficult decisions in the early days of establishing a collaborative team is important.

iii) Also, it is alright to review decisions and to make changes to help a collaborative relationship work better.

iv) For the school or setting to have a clear definition of what a collaborative teaching team means to them/their school; what it should look like? And what the success measure is for the school?

v) Pupils with diverse needs still require more resources. A collaborative team does not solve the learning needs for these pupils and teachers do need the support of class assistants, internal specialists and extra equipment to make their plans successful for these pupils.

This case study provides not only a real picture of how great team working and learning can impact positively on pedagogy, but also the complexities of collaboration. The words and phrases highlighted in the section above show the importance of interpersonal skills and of professional confidence to challenge and offer opinions appropriately. Importantly for the focus of this chapter it acknowledges that pupils with additional/diverse needs still require additional and different resources and input, to enable their success, despite the possible additional positives of varied teacher relationships, individualized programmes and greater whole staff understanding of their needs.

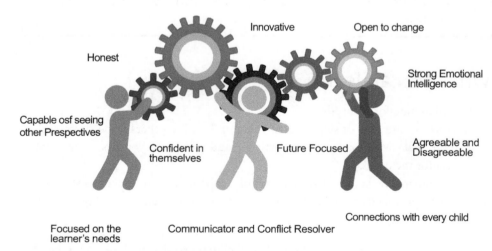

Figure 7.1 Key skills and dispositions of a collaborative teacher.

From the reflections of the participant (Eddie) in this case study you can see that for effective collaboration to happen each member of the partnership or group needs to have had the opportunity to develop and/or practice a range of interpersonal and professional skills. For some of you many of these will come quite naturally, but for other great teachers, the thought of challenging another colleague's opinion or way of working could be very difficult. It is also clearly paramount that the learning needs of all pupils must lead all collaborations and therefore it is important that as a teacher you are able to see your role and your responsibility to work in an inclusive manner whatever a pupil's additional need might be.

Reflective questions

1. Do you think you have the interpersonal and professional skills to work collaboratively?
2. If not, how do you think you can gain these skills?

Reflexive question

Do you feel you have any experiences or views that might impact on the way you work with pupils with autism, for example, or those who are highly able?

Critically engage with these experiences or views and consider how they might impact on your ability to work positively and inclusively with pupils with these needs.

The diagram (Figure 7.2) illustrates some 'Top Tips for Collaborating Teachers.' This hopefully will remind you of the key skills and dispositions of a collaborative teacher.

Working collaboratively with other professionals from different disciplines

It is important at this juncture to situate 'inclusive education' and 'inclusion' within this discussion about working together and collaboration. Although it originated in the 1800s, inclusion became reinvigorated in the second half of the twentieth century and it was the signing of the Salamanca Agreement (UNESCO, 1994) and The Dakar Agreement (UNESCO, 2000) that really influenced the direction of travel in government legislation in the UK and other countries such as the United States and Canada (Lynch and Irvine, 2009). Then and now these agreements and others

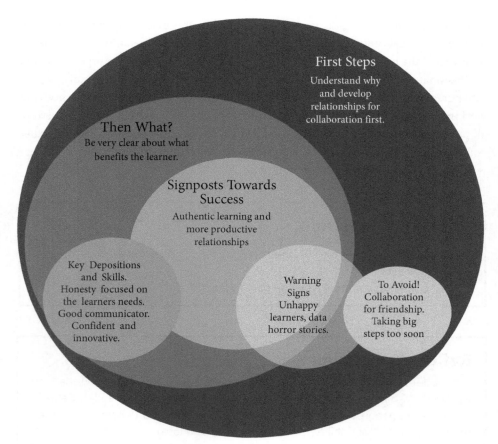

Figure 7.2 Top tips for collaborating teachers.

like the 'The UN Convention on the rights of the child' (UNICEF, 1989: Article 29) committed world leaders to the agreement that 'education must develop every child's personality, talents and abilities to the full', thus linking tightly to the ideology of inclusion. As yet no one definition of inclusion and inclusive education is generally agreed, but it is universally accepted that it constantly needs to change and respond to the individual needs of all pupils and not just those with special educational needs. If teachers work in an inclusive school therefore differences in learning and social need should be celebrated and valued (Corbett and Slee, 2000) and as Glazzard states (2014, p. 40), '[*inclusion*] *challenges educational settings to make adaptations and adjustments to cater for the needs of diverse learning. The purpose of inclusion is to provide all learners with equality of educational opportunity and this right is guaranteed through equality legislation'*. Whilst in agreement with Glazzard, we would add that any decision made must be led by pupil need with regard to community, curriculum and environment.

Reflective questions

1. What does 'inclusive education' mean to you and why?
2. In your personal or professional experience has pupil need(s) been central to all discussions? How has this impacted on your view of inclusion and thus on your practice?

When considering the role of inclusive practice with a particular focus on pupils with often complex additional physical, academic or social and emotional needs requiring specialist input from health or care professionals, discussion cannot remain enclosed within the arena of education, but requires the involvement of others from across society. Thus, across the last four or so decades, with the growing complexities of children and families' needs, national policies in many countries have constantly promoted the integration of services and joint working between disciplines and professionals (e.g. Anning et al., 2010; Edmond and Price, 2012). However, the actual impact of joint working on practice between teachers, health professionals (e.g. speech and language therapists, paediatricians, occupational therapists) and social care (plus many others) seems to be an ongoing cause for concern. Reasons offered for why this might be the case are many. Indeed, there are different models describing inter-professional collaborations, and statutory agencies continue to have separate funding streams, different employers and different working expectations, procedures and standards, all of which suggest a conflict between collaborative working ideals and actual practice. In 2013, Nancarrow et al. carried out a thematic synthesis of literature which identified some of the important components of collaborative working. Team working was found to be a particularly significant factor 'including the importance of respecting and understanding others' roles' (Soan, in Schuelka et al., 2019, p. 312). Earlier work (e.g. APPG, 2012; Cross, 2004; Soan, 2013; Soan, ibid.) endorse Nancarrow et al.'s (2013) findings, saying that 'professionals from different disciplines [are] focused on fulfilling the requirements determined by their own professional system and boundaries, which were also frequently constrained by budget and other resource factors rather than on the needs of the children'.

At this point I think I can hear you saying, 'Why and how is this of interest to me, a tutor, class teacher or senior leader?' To help you reflect on why this is all of importance to you, consider the following questions.

Reflective questions

1. When a pupil needs the input from an occupational therapist (OT) or speech and language therapist, how do you work together? Are you working for the same outcomes and are your discussions focused on the needs of the pupil or on other factors?

2. Now think back to the key skills and dispositions shared as outcomes of the research described in the case study about Eddie. Do you think you demonstrate all or some of these in this situation? Why, why not?

The following case study models how a class teacher can work effectively in collaboration with other professionals, putting the pupil at the centre of everyone's actions and sharing a common goal or outcome.

Case study: A collaboration with other professionals

Country: England

Age group: 13 years old (Year 8) comprehensive

Setting: A mainstream urban school

Participants involved: One teacher (in the first year of teaching); Ellen, a female pupil who was very able particularly in mathematics and science; a school counsellor; a university lecturer; the pupil's parents; and a charity (+forum).

The case study

Ellen had been at her secondary school for just over a year. She had returned to school following the summer holidays to find out that although she was still in the top streams (e.g. sets) for all her mathematics and science lessons, she had all new teachers who didn't appear to understand how she liked to learn. Ellen's favourite lesson was mathematics and her Year 7 teacher had, on recognizing her ability in the subject, provided her with work which enabled her to extend and deepen her knowledge and understanding. Unfortunately, this teacher had left the school. Ellen and her new form tutor had a positive relationship and so this teacher became concerned when after about seven weeks of the new school year, Ellen was beginning to be identified by many of her teachers as difficult, rude and defiant, and refusing to complete set tasks. There were also rumours from her peer group that Ellen was self-harming and isolating herself from her peer group. The teacher's concerns were further heightened when data showed Ellen's grades had fallen substantially and she was not meeting any of her target expectations. During a progress review meeting with the Year Head and the Inclusion Manager (this role will also usually incorporate the role of the SENCO in England), Ellen's changing learning and behaviour profile was discussed.

The form teacher (with the Year Head's support) was asked to carry out further investigations as it was clear Ellen was not progressing well. The form tutor started by observing Ellen working in her mathematics class and then set up a meeting with Ellen's parents and also Ellen herself. Even though she was in her first year of teaching this teacher had recognized the importance of collaboration and communication. Following this a meeting with the Head of Mathematics and her subject teacher was arranged. Finally, the form tutor met with Ellen again and discussed with her what she had managed to organize. Through careful listening, observations and talking to all parties involved with Ellen, the form tutor had identified that Ellen felt as if she was a failure as she had not been enabled to progress at her normal rate and this had caused her to become depressed and anxious (leading to self-harming), not wanting to mix with her peers or even attend her usually most popular subject lessons. With her Senior Leaders agreement and in partnership with the subject teachers, Ellen and her parents, additional specialist support was put in place and a collaborative action plan centred around Ellen's needs was put in place. The common goal was to enable Ellen to feel as if she was making good academic progress and to regain the confidence in her own ability. Figure 7.3 shows who was involved and how with a commonly agreed outcome professionals used their specialist knowledge to meet Ellen's individual learning and emotional needs.

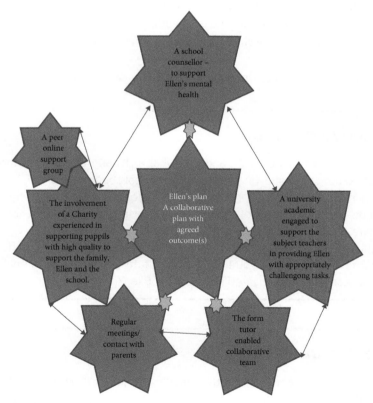

Figure 7.3 Ellen's collaborative plan.

Outcomes

1. The collaborative partnership provided Ellen with the support needed (academically and emotionally) to re-establish positive self-esteem and provide a challenging, well-supported individualized curriculum.
2. Ellen stopped getting into trouble with staff members.
3. Ellen stopped self-harming.
4. Ellen's progress was positive.

What we can learn

1. The form tutor did not assume that Ellen's changing behaviour was someone else's responsibility, but also recognized she needed to work collaboratively.
2. The form tutor demonstrated excellent listening and observation skills, not making assumptions, but taking time to talk, listen and observe all involved with the pupil. (For more information on this read Chapter 6.)
3. The form tutor also showed she was willing to collaborate with others (as the subject teachers did as well) who had specialist knowledge – in the best interest of the pupil.
4. Collaborative working is not a 'quick fix', but it can be life-changing.

Reflective questions

1. Thinking back to Figures 7.1 and 7.2, what skills and abilities did the form tutor demonstrate showing her strengths in collaborative working?
2. If you had a pupil with SEN or high ability who was not coping, what would you do (within your school's budget and access to specialists of course) to ensure they were fully included.
3. Return to the list of skills and positive dispositions emboldened on page 13. How many of these do you think the form tutor probably had to enable her to carry out this personalized approach for Ellen?

Reflexive questions

1. Have you learnt anything about yourself and your inclusive practice from reading this case study?
2. How will your reflections enhance your practice?

This case study has shown how powerful effective joint working/collaboration can be for all teachers working with pupils with special educational needs and those who are able, gifted or/and talented. All action was centred around the pupil's needs and provided each specialist professional to carry out their work with one jointly held plan. Think of all the hours of detentions, the threat of exclusion, lost education and anxious professionals and parents avoided by this form tutor through her determination to ensure she found out what was the barrier(s) to Ellen's behaviour and lack of engagement in learning.

Working with professionals from other disciplines for inclusive practice development

Window on research

Hutton, E., and Soan, S. (2015). '"Lessons Learned" from introducing universal strategies designed to support the motor and functional skills of Reception and Year 1 children in a sample of primary schools in South East England', *Education, 3–13, pp: 1–21. Available at:* http://dx.doi.org/10.1080/03004279.2015.1048270

The window on research detailed here provides information about how teachers working collaboratively with other professionals, Occupational Therapists, gained new knowledge and skills, and vice versa. The research also clearly demonstrates how issues might arise between different professionals when common outcomes focused on the needs of pupils are not agreed before collaborative work begins.

This research was an evaluation of novel universal resources, designed by a special educational needs specialist and an occupational therapist, to support motor development in Reception (4–5-year-olds) and Year 1 (5–6-year-olds) pupils. The research took place in four schools in the South-East of England, three of which had high numbers of pupils considered disadvantaged, over a period of twelve weeks. The take up of the initiative was influenced by senior leadership engagement. The initiative also contributed to a national programme's targets (Healthy Schools).

Using a qualitative methodology, interviews and focus group, data were collected alongside pupils' schoolwork.

The researchers found that at the end of the twelve-week intervention period pupils' sitting, handwriting and lunchtime skills had improved, warranting further and larger-scale research of this approach aimed at addressing pupils' motor skills needs on school entry.

Not surprisingly one finding was that teachers were most interested in the resources that had the greatest focus on teaching and learning. Even though the resources were framed as 'universal' it was evident from the findings that strategies still needed to be supplied to teachers with quite detailed information. In addition, support from either a specialist educator or occupational therapist was required to enable teachers to understand the principles and theories that underpinned the strategies. School-based or community occupational therapists adopted a collaborative approach to this sharing of knowledge with the class teachers. With ongoing access to advice and support, teachers were able to accept daily responsibility for movement and coordination development work alongside their health colleagues. They shared a common goal and desired outcome.

The importance of keeping the pupils' needs central and having a common outcome target was further magnified by identified study limitations. Occupational therapy students unused to working with large groups of children and a number of professionals struggled initially with the new environment, finding it difficult to gather the data they needed for their own studies. Additionally, the Healthy Schools team members' perception of their role and the study became entangled when the information they needed to meet their targets were not forthcoming. This prompted the researchers to reflect on how to implement universal strategies in schools and the requirement for support when sharing specialist knowledge (Godemann, 2008), noting the importance of the collaborative skills required and an outcome all agree with from the beginning of any work. Despite these limitations the study did demonstrate that there are opportunities to collaborate on targets/outcomes relating to health and well-being across disciplines and professions (O'Toole and Kirkpatrick, 2007). Finally, findings were felt to indicate that jointly developed resources (between health and education professionals) might assist collaborative working, overcoming professional culture and language (Kennedy and Stewart, 2011).

Although only a small-scale research, this study concurs with findings from the literature and other research and case studies discussed throughout this chapter.

Using the case studies and the Window on research make a list of the aspects you feel you can with careful reflection enhance in your own practice.

Reflective questions

1. Having read this chapter and reflected on the information included, can you see how collaborative working and the co-joined-required skills can help you as you continue to develop your inclusive practice?
2. Can you recognize the benefits of working in effective collaborative partnerships when working with pupils with special educational needs and those with high ability and talents?

> **Reflexive question**
>
> Reviewing your initial feelings and views about collaboration, has the practice examples in this chapter helped you gain confidence in your practice alongside the understanding that inclusion of all pupils is every teacher's responsibility and role?

Conclusion

As expressed in all of the chapters in this book in many different ways, understanding your own strengths and dispositions is crucial if you are going to grow/continue to grow and develop in your teaching career. This chapter has chiefly explored and illustrated that working together is not as easy as legislation and policy often suggest and that the factors and skills required to establish collaborative team working, whether with other teachers or other professionals from different disciplines, need the pupil to be at the centre of all decision-making and clear jointly held outcomes. It has also provided you with the types of interpersonal skills necessary to be able to work in a true collaborative manner and challenges you to think about which ones (if any) you need support with developing further.

Many pupils with special educational needs, DME or who are able and talented will need a collaborative approach if they are going to fulfil their own expectations and hopes and it is every teacher's personal, social and emotional responsibility to enable this as best they can.

Implications for educators

1. Inclusion, for all pupils, is every teacher's responsibility.
2. Collaborative practice needs time and space, so school leaders need to recognize that it is not a 'quick fix' approach but is worth the effort in the long run.
3. Teachers need to have support and supervision to identify, acknowledge and then develop areas of their practice which will help them enhance their inclusive practice and working together with others.
4. Consideration needs to be given when working with professionals from other disciplines about their need to meet their own standards and regulations whilst also meeting the needs of the pupil(s) and education colleagues.
5. Interpersonal skills and collaborative working need to be practised and developed whilst teachers (and others) receive their initial training and this needs to be ongoing throughout a teacher's career.

6. Working together should not be a luxury, but an essential so that all pupils with additional and often complex needs can access specialist knowledge and skills across a range of disciplines on a regular and ongoing way.

Annotated bibliography

Anning, A., Cottrell, D., Frost, N., Green, J. and Robinson, M. (2010). *Developing multiprofessional teamwork for integrated children's services.* **Maidenhead: Open University Press.**
This is a book which focuses its attention on integrated practice, specifically in England. However, it has wider appeal with its informative guidance, theoretical frameworks and evidence-based insights into practice and is therefore a useful resource for all student teachers, beginning and more experienced teachers, social workers and support workers.

Edmond, N. and Price, M. (2012). *Integrated working with children and young people: Supporting development from birth to nineteen.* **London: Sage.**
This is an introduction to many issues discussed in this book providing additional information on how to manage working with families, professionalism, transitions and many more areas connected to inclusive practice.

Soan, S. and ACT colleagues (2019). 'Multi-disciplinary practice and inclusive education', in Schuelka, M., Thomas, G., Johnstone, C. and Artiles, A. (eds.) *SAGE handbook of inclusion and diversity in education.* **London: Sage.**
This is essential reading for all who want to understand more about inclusion and diversity in education. It has many contributions in chapters from across the globe considering issues from a global to a local level. It is divided into three sections:
Part I is about Conceptualizations and possibilities of inclusion and diversity in education followed in Part II with a look at education practices, policies and systems. The final section Part III includes chapters about disability, diversity and inclusion from all parts of the world.

8

Resilience, Reflection and Reflexivity

Geraldene Codina and Jon Fordham

Introduction

Historically the teacher resilience literature has tended to focus on the individual (Day, 2017), their ability to manage stressors and risk factors and to draw on protective factors (Howard and Johnson, 2004). More recently the emphasis has shifted from analysis of the individual towards understandings which emphasize the interaction between individuals and their environments (Ungar, 2012). Focused more on the latter rather than the former, this chapter moves away from the potentially damaging effects of a 'pull yourself together' mentality, in favour of analysis which contextualizes teacher resilience. Teacher resilience is viewed more in terms of the space where an individual's capacity to navigate challenges interacts over time with their personal and professional contexts (Beltman, 2015). The desired outcome of this meeting between individual and context is a teacher who experiences professional engagement and growth, commitment, enthusiasm, satisfaction, and well-being (Beltman, 2015) and thus is able to act in a personally, socially and emotionally responsible way. It is the intention of this chapter to encourage you to examine your own professional resilience, reflexivity and reflection and thus grow in your understanding about how to teach all pupils whatever their needs made be. It is particularly in this way this chapter aligns with professional experiences discussed earlier in this book (e.g. see Chapters 2, 3 and 7). The nexus between professional challenge and teacher satisfaction is also explored through two case studies presented in this chapter and the subsequent discussion which addresses the inclusion of children with diverse needs (both special educational needs and/or disability (SEND) and able and talented).

Reflection and reflexive practice emerge in this chapter as two key components of resilience. Much is written about both topics and 'many models, frameworks or theories describe reflective and reflexive processes' (Bolton with Delderfield, 2018, p. 52). For the purposes of this chapter, 'reflection' is broadly defined as the action of purposefully thinking about education so as to improve professional practice (Sellars, 2017). This might involve the rational, logical analysis of a problem (Dewey, 1933) or could occur 'in action' whilst a problem is being addressed (Schön, 1983). Reflection will always be 'for action' (i.e. for a purpose) (Eraut, 1995), but need not be triggered by negative events or positioned around a problem (Boud, Keogh and Walker, 1985). Returning to the Latin-derived definition, 'reflexivity' refers to a turning back on oneself. Reflexivity concerns developing one's self-awareness of what we bring to a situation, having an awareness of the capital that can influence actions, the habits which can become unquestioningly assumed and the nature of the field in which we operate (Bourdieu with Wacquant, 1992). As such it involves 'question[ing] our own attitudes, theories-in-use, values, assumptions, prejudices and habitual actions; to understand our complex roles in relation to others' (Bolton with Delderfield, 2018, p. 10). A teacher's reflexive awareness should therefore shape their in-action reflections; that is, the in-the-moment choices teachers make concerning interactions with others (colleagues, parents, children etc.). Of central importance to this chapter is the position reflection and reflexive action play with regard to valuing diversity and promoting inclusion for those described as having additional needs. As with other chapters in this book, teachers' personal, social and emotional responsibility will be highlighted throughout this chapter.

The two case studies presented in this chapter are viewed as the narrative which shapes the direction of the discussion and analysis. Involving five people, the case studies are a small-scale sample and are not intended to be representative of a universal experience. Rather the case studies are utilized as a way to connect theory to practising teachers' lived experiences (van Manen, 1900) of the three Rs: resilience, reflection and reflexive action. The aim of the chapter is to share with you other teachers' experiences of these three Rs (and others), so you can reflexively consider their actions in relation to your own 'professional becoming' (Dall'Alba, 2009). It is acknowledged that professional becoming is not a straightforward matter, but rather involves ambiguities, such as possible options, combined with a certain number of constraints (Dall'Alba, 2009).

Case study: 1

Country: England

Age group: 4–11 years

Setting: A government-funded mainstream school which is statistically described as being in a City where social mobility is low. The inclusion statement in the English National Curriculum (DfE, 2014, p. 9) requires all teachers to 'set high expectations for every pupil. They should plan stretching work for pupils whose attainment is significantly above the expected standard, [and] they have an even greater obligation to plan lessons for pupils who have low levels of prior attainment or come from disadvantaged backgrounds'.

Participants involved: Four teachers (three qualified teachers and one Newly Qualified Teacher)

The case study

Since 2013 the school has worked to develop its vision for pupils in the setting, a key mission being pupils understand, believe in and achieve their full potential. This is lived through resilience, resourcefulness, reflectiveness and reciprocity (from now called the four Rs). Of their own volition, staff take personal responsibility to further emphasize the four Rs in their own classrooms through the use of class mottos, such as: 'I'm always proud of you if you try', 'the more you put in the more you get out', 'see if you can try just a little bit harder' etc. When defining resilience, staff refer to perseverance and motivation; this applies to both themselves and the pupils. Engagement with challenge is unanimously described by participants as the mechanism for achieving higher levels of resilience.

When referring to their own personal challenges, the group spoke not of anxiety, isolation or fear, but of working with others (reciprocity) to maintain their own interest levels and as a way to gain support.

The group's description of their social responsibility to work in a collegiate way can be analysed as three pronged: whole school/team, individual and informal.

Whole school/team

Continuing Professional Development (CPD) which leads to practise change; for example, at the whole school level CPD has addressed teaching to age-related expectations and the implementation of a new maths scheme which supports deep understanding. Engagement with research is also a prominent part of the whole school culture. Staffs' personal responsibility to engage with research takes on many forms; for example, reading and discussing research in a weekly focused research meeting, drawing on published research as the basis for teaching, conducting small-scale research, disseminating their own research findings and publishing research.

Individualized coaching and mentoring are a key part of the school's enhancement strategy. With many staff in the school trained to coach colleagues, mechanisms are in place to empower staff to work collaboratively with one another to solve challenges. For example, one coach spoke about discussing with a coachee-teacher ways to remove barriers for a child with speech and communication needs. The process of coaching helped the teacher reflect upon the current situation and recall a previous time when the coachee removed barriers for a pupil with complex needs on the SEN register. Drawing on this previous experience the coachee decided she needed to work further on her relationship with the pupil, gaining a deeper understanding of the pupil's likes and dislikes. This information was subsequently utilized as the basis for personalizing work, whilst also meeting the school's requirement to teach to age-related expectations.

Informal conversations between staff; for example, staff spoke of a culture of open, honest communication that regularly involved sharing successes related to pupil's learning and reflecting with a colleague when pupils seem more challenged by a specific concept.

On the theme of challenge, the group described a need to balance the new with the familiar. Too much challenge can become overwhelming, potentially depleting a person's resilience rather than building it. Crucially, staff spoke of the importance of working in an appreciation culture. This culture is embedded through varied means, such as formalized mechanisms (i.e. observation), to less formalized encounters when staff take time to genuinely thank people for their individualized efforts or celebrate successes together.

Continuing with the theme of collaboration, the group spoke about their emotional and social responsibility to respect others' ways of working, and of their personal responsibility to look after themselves as professionals (i.e. understanding what depletes their resilience and conversely what restores it). Referring to their emotional and social responsibility to others, staff described the importance of knowing others'/their own stressors; organization and work ethic emerged as two key discussion topics. The effect of these forms of personal, social and emotional awareness is a general raising of professional teachers' standards and a reduction in stress levels; for example, getting work completed the evening before so colleagues with childcare commitments do not have too much to organize first thing in the morning. Reflexively focusing on their own in-the-moment decisions and actions, staff considered whether the intended impact of their actions was in fact the impact felt by others. Referring to their personal responsibility to look after their own well-being, staff spoke of knowing how to ensure they each have time away from the job (i.e. some spoke of working a longer day, but not taking work home; others described having a specific allocated time at the weekend when they prepared for the following week etc.).

Outcomes

The school has developed its own inclusive culture which means all pupils and staff alike feel able to thrive and achieve. When problems arise, staff feel able to raise these and work collaboratively to solve issues. Over the past 5 years the school's inspectorate judgement (made by Ofsted, the Inspection Body in England) has improved from 'inadequate' to 'good'.

Reflective and reflexive questions

Focusing specifically on the inclusion of pupils described as having additional needs, consider the following reflective and reflexive questions.

1. Referring to building and enhancing their resilience, the teachers involved described: challenge, working in a collegiate way, engagement with research, and honest open discussions as key factors. *Reflecting on your own personal experience, what would you describe as building your professional resilience?*
2. The teachers described the multiple ways they reflect on their professional day; for example, through whole school CPD, coaching, engagement with research and informal conversations with colleagues. *What strategies do you have for reflecting on the working day and how does this reflection impact on the next day/future?*

The teachers reflexively considered the intended impact of their own professional actions versus the actual impact felt by others. Over time this reflexivity has led to an increased understanding of their social and emotional responsibilities to others, their personal responsibility to themselves, and their personal and emotional drivers. As such, staff have become more aware of their own professional habits and the motives which drive their actions. Staff describe the importance of learning good habits from one another and also their social responsibility to accommodate other colleagues' needs. This high-level personal, social and emotional awareness facilitates a school environment where:

- staff work together to ensure pupils are included and making progress;
- staff feel able to articulate their professional needs, learn good habits from others and make adjustments to their practice which support others' personal resilience.

Reflexive questions

Focusing on your own professional actions in the moment, especially when working with pupils with special educational needs or/and who are highly able/talented, can you reflexively analyse:

1. What personal and emotional drivers impact your decision making – i.e. what are the motivators powering your actions?

2. What actions have you taken which you subsequently adjusted, or would like to adjust? How have/could these adjustments impact your ability to be resilient?
3. Whether the intended impact of your actions is the same as the impact felt by others?

Case study: 2

Country: Hong Kong

Age group: 3–18 years

Setting:
A private international school. Private international schools adopt a more Western culture of education, focusing on pupil well-being alongside academic excellence. Private schooling is expensive but an important option for families whose children do not speak Cantonese or Mandarin.

Participants involved:
The Deputy Head of the international primary school (Jay[1]).

The case study

Jay describes the school as following a holistic approach to education. The school's philosophy is around the development of the whole child, providing the opportunity for individuals to pursue their strengths and interests alongside developing their curiosity, independence, confidence and resilience. Ensuring that pupils have life skills forms part of the curriculum entitlement and this requires a deep understanding of each pupil. When developing resilience in pupils, the school's starting point is always to understand the whole person, knowing their strengths, interests and what motivates them. Teachers then plan opportunities for pupils to experience 'failure' or 'losing' in a structured and supportive environment so they can apply the strategies taught. Initially, when identifying a group of pupils with lower levels of resilience, the most able were found to be those in greatest need of support. However, further analysis revealed a sub-group within the main group who are classed as twice exceptional. These pupils are described as highly intelligent but who may struggle in school due to a disability or learning difference – i.e. dyslexia, autism or trauma. As a result, the disability may conceal their gifts and pupils may find school difficult and become frustrated. Discussion with this group revealed they have an extreme fear of failure, which results in giving up easily or not wanting to try. This experience further motivated staff in the school to ensure they taught resilience as part of the curriculum.

---

[1] Jay is not the teacher's real name but is rather a pseudonym used to maintain her anonymity.

When referring to her own resilience, Jay describes working in a school culture which understands change is inevitable and thus is open to it and better prepared. Alongside this acceptance, staff find holding themselves and others to high professional standards ensures clear expectations for the results they desire. There is an acceptance that events will occur which deplete resilience, but that the reflective process which takes place afterwards is essential for restoring resilience for next time. This cycle of challenge, reflection and resilience is described as preparing staff in the setting for future challenges. Jay also identified reflection as a process that can happen in different timescales; for example, reflecting in the moment when your questioning has not engaged all pupils, or deeper reflections occurring after sessions which focus on alternative strategies to engage pupils. Similarly, this applies to professional dialogues such as a lull in a staff meeting, or reflecting later about a conversation with a member of staff. She also highlighted the importance of gaining feedback or liaising with other members of staff to support this reflective process.

Jay acknowledged when making challenging decisions awareness of her emotional drivers and that of other staff was important. She quoted Patrick Lencioni's work on the *Five Dysfunctions of a Team* as a personal driver to support making difficult decisions. These are: absence of trust, fear of conflict, lack of commitment, avoidance of accountability and inattention results.

When considering professional development, Jay identified two examples where her practice moved on the quickest. The first was the demand of needing to be an 'expert' in an area within a short timescale which motivated her to take time to research and distil key points in a meaningful and relevant way to other staff. The other was through the use of 360-degree Feedback surveys. Through this honest professional feedback, Jay was given a 'safe place' to explore her areas for development and have coaching discussions to identify strategies to tackle them with a trusted professional.

Jay describes challenge as the main driver for developing her resilience. She views it as a driver for reflection in the moment and after the event. To make the right decision, however, is a combination of knowing yourself and others and working in a culture of openness-to-feedback and collaboration with others.

Outcomes

- Analysis of data for pupils with additional needs resulted in the group being further supported to develop their resilience.
- Challenge led to rapid practice development for Jay.
- Consultation with others provided Jay with a 'safe place' to explore her areas for development. Coaching provided the means to work on development areas.

Reflective and reflexive questions

Focusing specifically on the inclusion of pupils described as having additional needs, consider the following reflective and reflexive questions.

1. In question 1 you identified actions which built your resilience, can you now think about what maintains and restores your resilience, and conversely what depletes your resilience?

2. Jay refers to a deep understanding of the whole child born of analysis as the main factor influencing her decision-making in the classroom. She also describes analysis with colleagues as shaping her understanding. Her understanding of the pupil is situated therefore in research and collaboration.

Regarding supporting/extending pupil's learning and resilience, what factors influence your decision-making in the classroom?

What we can learn

There are many points presented in the case studies above which could be drawn out and interpreted as to their meaning (Gadamer, 1998, pp. 66–8); however, for the purposes of this chapter the following themes will be explored: change, challenge and uncertainty, and whole-school values and collaboration. To support your engagement with the chapter, key questions relevant to your own professional becoming (Dall'Alba, 2009) are presented throughout the discussion.

Personal and emotional responsibility: Change, challenge and uncertainty

All five participants featured in the case studies perceived there to be a correlation between resilience and an ability to handle change and challenge. We have been careful not to refer specifically to the individual's ability to be resilient or handle change and challenge, for it is argued that resilience occurs in a context (Beltman, 2015), dependent on both the characteristics of the situation as well as the characteristics of a teacher (Kennedy, 2010). Reflexively analysing the need for teachers to manage change brings into view the field of teaching (Bourdieu with Wacquant, 1992) which is imbued with uncertainty (Helsing, 2007). For example, there is no one correct pedagogy or 'the' approved theory for educating the able and talented; inclusion has no one agreed definition and is even argued to be inconsistently implemented at the level of a single country's governmental policy (Hodkinson, 2016). Such uncertainties point to a profession which operates in an interpretivistic rather than positivistic paradigm. This is perhaps not surprising as teaching is a job which predominantly relies on the forming of human relationships with trust, respect and authenticity. Arguably those teachers who 'remain in the profession with motivation and commitment have learned to handle this kind of uncertainty in a positive manner' (Kroll, 2012, p. 19). Even the nature of this uncertainty is contested; for example, is it a liability or an asset? (Helsing, 2007).

Your professional becoming

What uncertainties have you encountered in education? How do you perceive and manage these uncertainties?

The teachers featured in case studies 1 and 2 are arguably those Kroll (2012) describes as having learned to handle this kind of uncertainty in a positive manner. Rather than referring to their classroom practice as fixed and defined, they each described their personal responsibility to know the pupils in their classes and respond to them as individuals. Those in case study 1 articulated this through the lens and language of a growth mindset (Dweck, 2015) – i.e. referring to the effort pupils make rather than a perception of pupil's innate talent or permanently fixed ability. Whereas Jay (case study 2) described her commitment to all pupils' holistic development and the importance of building pupils' resilience (Claxton, 2018). The participants' analysis of each pupil as an individual with their own strengths, talents and ability is particularly significant to the context of this book for it maps onto Booth and Ainscow's (2011) inclusive pedagogy for *all*. Emphasizing the importance of participation, Booth and Ainscow's (2011) construction of inclusion refers to learning, playing or working in collaboration with others; making choices about, and having a say in, what happens; and being recognized and accepted for oneself. Of particular note is the wide-reaching nature of this statement, for it includes all those in the school community: children and adults. This construction of inclusion will be referred to in more detail in the conclusion to this chapter.

What other constructions of inclusion have you encountered? How does Booth and Ainscow's (2011) construction of inclusion compare to others you are aware of?

Analysis of the case study participants' inclusive beliefs (Booth and Ainscow, 2011) about pupil ability/disability suggests their construction of learners is more interventionist in nature, rather than pathognomonic (Jordan, Schwartz and McGhie-Richmond, 2009). Teachers who have a strong interventionist perspective generally think about pupils in terms of how they learn best, whereas those holding a pathognomonic perspective are more likely to focus on the pathological characteristics of the learner – i.e. a within pupil construction ability/disability as a fixed entity. The interventionist focus on 'context for learning' aligns closely with a social model view of disability, where the aim is to remove environmental barriers, rather than adjust and remediate the 'disabled person' (Oliver, 2004). Conversely pathognomonic perspectives correlate more closely with a biological, medical model perspective of disability and thus tend to adopt the language of symptoms, disorders and treatment. Reflexive analysis (Bourdieu with Wacquant, 1992) of the medical model points to a need for specialist assessments, a special pedagogy, specialist knowledge and/or qualifications, specialist intervention, etc. Reviewing the teaching practice of those in Jordan, Schwartz and McGhie-Richmond's (2009) study with a pathognomonic perspective also reveals a correlation between their beliefs and medical model practice. For example, they were more likely to believe in segregated forms of pupil intervention, not recognizing their personal responsibility to educate all pupils in their class, and to feel they themselves were not sufficiently qualified to teach pupils with a label of Special Educational Needs and Disability. It was also shown these teachers had less effective practice overall (e.g. time management and classroom management). Interestingly, in a separate paper (also from Canada), Gray, Wilcox and Nordstokke (2017) align depleted teacher resilience with the growing trend towards inclusive education. Appearing to take a different stance on inclusion to Booth and Ainscow (2016), Gray, Wilcox and Nordstokke's (2017) analysis suggests a more pathognomonic perspective which emphasizes specialized SEND knowledge and points to studies which argue teaching pupils with SEN creates less time for the rest of the class.

Reflecting on your own teaching practice, would you describe yourself as more aligned with the interventionist or pathognomonic perspective? How does this effect your interactions/the support you provide for pupils with additional needs?

Analysis of the literature pertaining to an inclusive pedagogy for pupils described as able and talented, unsurprisingly, also tends to reject segregation of able pupils from their peers (Hymer and Michel, 2002; Moltzen, 2011, 2006). For some the argument leads to a focus on in-class enrichment over early participation in a curriculum pupils will have access to in the fullness of time (Hymer and Michel, 2002), whereas for others like Moltzen (2011) the picture is less clear. An ongoing issue highlighted in the literature is the challenge of defining what is meant by able and talented and to whom it pertains (Sternberg, 2019). The heterogeneous nature of the able and talented group points to the complexity of this label and the tension in the literature. A heterogenous construction of able and talented mirrors the viewpoints of participants in this study who spoke of recognizing the many different ways pupils could be viewed as able (from ability in a subject, to skills-based abilities like being a resilient learner). Once again, the teachers spoke of a fluid rather than fixed perception of pupil ability, describing no one pupil as able in every aspect of learning (Moltzen, 2006) and some pupils as twice exceptional (i.e. both able and with a special educational need). The challenge for teachers in removing barriers and engaging the latter is that twice exceptional learners can become invisible to teachers, as ability in one area can mask disability in another (Silverman, 2019).

Do you perceive pupil's ability to be fluid or fixed? How is your belief about pupil's ability exemplified in your teaching practice?

Perceiving pupil's ability as fixed (akin with constructs of IQ) and holding pathognomonic beliefs about SEN might lead to some of the following school behaviours and cultures:

1. Teachers expressing a view that certain pupils with SEND are not suited to their class or should not be part of their school, perhaps being more suited to a special segregated education where they will receive 'expert treatment'.
2. Pupils with SEND spending significant amounts of time away from their peer group in intervention groups or perhaps even in isolation rooms.
3. Pressure from parent groups for certain pupils with SEND (particularly affecting behaviour) to be excluded from a school.
4. Teaching assistants spending greater proportions of time with pupils with a label of SEND than qualified teachers.
5. Increased applications for additional funding for pupils who have SEN.
6. Teachers undervaluing and failing to recognize ability in pupils whose aptitudes lie outside the boundaries of a curriculum subject.
7. Teachers failing to recognize ways to remove barriers and enable twice exceptional pupils.

It is important to recognize the school behaviours described above can happen for a number of different reasons. Thus, careful reflexive analysis (Bourdieu with Wacquant, 1992) of a school's behaviour is required before conclusions can be drawn regarding the nature of a school's actions.

Reflexive questions

1. The behaviours described above are rarely the result of one person's actions, rather more commonly result from a complex range of factors. Can you reflexively analyse the possible factors leading to such behaviours?
2. How might these factors be addressed within a school? Your answer is likely to require an interweaving of possibility with constraint (Dall'Alba, 2009), possibility of what could happen, woven together with the structural constraint of what can happen.

Social responsibility: Whole school values and collaboration

There has been much debate in the literature about the nature of resilience and whether or not an individual's personal survival characteristics and their ability to be super-human have been overly focused upon (Day and Gu, 2014; Margolis and Alexandrou, 2014). Whilst this debate remains unresolved, there is consensus in the literature that context counts (Day and Gu, 2014; Margolis and Alexandrou, 2014); this analysis echoes narratives presented in both case studies featured in this chapter. Case studies 1 and 2 include descriptions concerning the process for building and maintaining resilience. Crucially in both instances this involves space for reflection, time for collaboration and perhaps, counter-intuitively, challenge.

Starting with challenge, whilst too much challenge holds the potential to damage resilience, being supported to accomplish new things, perhaps even actions perceived as difficult, is described in both case studies as the mechanism for building resilience. Mapping this onto teaching and learning, there is a parallel here between the case study descriptions of building resilience and Vygotsky's theory (1962) on the zone of proximal development (ZPD); that is, with good support and scaffolding the teachers featured in case studies 1 and 2 have been able to meet the challenging personal, social and emotional responsibilities associated with being a school teacher. Returning to the concept of uncertainty in education (Helsing, 2007), it is perhaps not surprising to find the case study participants describing ongoing learning as an essential component to maintaining their personal resilience.

Reflective questions

1. Can you think of a time when you have been supported to achieve a challenge?
2. How did this experience build your resilience?

It is interesting to note that reflection is clearly present in all participants' analyses of resilience; in both case studies coaching is identified as a tool for reflection. Coaching can take on a number of formats from informal to specialist, self-coaching to team coaching and collaborative peer-coaching (Wharton et al., 2019). In case study 1 setting, teachers and teaching assistants all have the opportunity to train as a coach, thus anyone in the school can approach a trained member of staff to gain personal support with a challenge they are analysing. The coacher avoids providing the answers for the coachee, rather engages them in a series of questions that facilitate reflection and reflexive action resulting in finding new ways to approach a situation. As described in case study 1, reflection of this nature can support inclusion and the valuing of diversity (Bolton with Delderfield, 2018), for it provides opportunity to enhance provision and meet the specific needs of individual pupils.

Your professional development

Can you think of a time when your professional resilience has been supported by working with others in a reflective way? What form did this reflection have (i.e. group collaboration in CPD, engagement with research, informal conversation etc.)? Can you think of a time when reflection has enabled you to value diversity and act inclusively?

For participants in both case studies, continued engagement with research is an essential part of their working lives. Staff in case study 1 described their continued engagement with research as a 'professional right', thus making research a part of their teacherly identity, whereas Jay described drawing on research as an important mechanism for moving her practice on quickly. This engagement is of fundamental importance, for it provides the basis for reflexive work, which enables the exploration of values, assumptions, prejudices and habitual actions (Bolton with Delderfield, 2018, p. 10). Reflexive work of this nature is also argued to provide a means to abate the discourse of 'expertism', where expertism constructs special education through the lens of pathologies requiring prescription outside the skill base of the mainstream teacher (Robinson, 2017). The significance of reflexive thinking is also highlighted in Kroll's (2012) analysis of Lambe and Bones's (2007) work with trainee teachers in Northern Ireland. For despite a trainee's successful experience working in a non-selective school which includes pupils with SEND and the trainees' change in attitudes towards ability grouping, they still held an intractable belief that they personally would not have done so well in a non-selective setting. Similarly, Charles's (2019) work into the employment of teachers with dyslexia in England reveals that whilst schools might operate an inclusive policy for the pupils in their setting, removing barriers for teaching staff with dyslexia is perceived as unreasonable. There are no easy solutions to the scenarios highlighted by Kroll (2012) and Charles (2019); however, they do point to a school's social responsibility to 'find a variety of methods for holding these beliefs up to inquiry and scrutiny' (Kroll, 2012, p. 80).

Your professional becoming

Can you think of a time when engagement with research has provided the basis for your own reflexive analysis? Can you think of opportunities for you to disseminate your engagement with research?

Window on research

Norwich, B., and Ylonen, A. (2014). 'Lesson study practices in the development of secondary teaching of students with moderate learning difficulties: A systematic qualitative analysis in relation to context and outcomes', *British Educational Research Journal*, 41(4), pp. 629–49.

The window on research detailed below provides another example of teachers' engagement with research to benefit pupils with additional needs.

Lesson study is an internationally known model of teacher-led practitioner research which aims to support professional development and facilitate reflective practice. Popular in Japan, the approach engages a small group of teachers in co-planning a cycle of research lessons (often three) involving review and development. Once co-planning is complete, one teacher from the group leads the lesson whilst the others observe. Feedback from the lesson studied focuses on student learning rather than teacher practice. Drawing on the observers' comments, together the team then develop and enhance the next lesson to be studied.

Whilst lesson study has generally focused on mathematics and science education, Norwich and Ylonen (2014) advance the research field by addressing the inclusion of pupils with moderate learning difficulties (MLD). In the paper referred to above, Norwich and Ylonen (2014) complete work with sixty-one school teachers from twenty-nine schools on lesson study. Norwich and Ylonen's (2014) research focused specifically on two main aims:

1. the variations of lesson study practice used by teachers; and
2. the extent to which teachers' context related to the efficacy of lesson study.

Norwich and Ylonen (2014) found teams adapted lesson study to suit their particular subject area, and the needs of pupils identified with Moderate Learning Difficulties (MLD) in their teaching contexts. Norwich and Ylonen (2014) argue these findings indicate the flexibility of lesson study; they do point out that whilst the teachers involved had been encouraged to use research-informed knowledge relevant to teaching pupils with MLD, this happened between 40 per cent and 50 per cent of the time. Teachers who did not refer to research-informed knowledge drew on their personal/craft knowledge and/or some more general research knowledge as the basis for shaping their decisions, the teachers interviewed for the research found this approach adequate. Teachers engaged in the study worked on aims that were both curriculum-focused and more general (e.g. development of pupil independence, enhancement of pupil engagement etc.). Analysis of the data shows how variations in the degree to which schools were supportive of lesson study (timing, release and management support) correlates positively with pupil learning gains and teacher outcomes, as well as a school's continued use of lesson study. Norwich and Ylonen (2014) argue these findings provide support for the model of lesson study depicted in their paper. If you are interested in lesson study, how would you construct a proposal to introduce it in your setting?

Conclusion

Teaching as a profession is argued to contain numerous uncertainties (Helsing, 2007) and as pointed to in this chapter, the fields of special education, able and talented and inclusion are no exception. Reflective and reflexive practices such as engagement with coaching, research and surveys can be viewed as tools of the interventionist paradigm (Jordan, Schwartz and McGhie-Richmond, 2009); tools which enable staff to meet the needs of the individual pupil and develop the whole child. Perhaps surprisingly, challenge emerges as the key component for building staff resilience; for example, a staff member describes a scenario where learning to meet the needs of a specific pupil with a label of SEN built their resilience. Challenge of this nature is however unlikely to be an efficacious resilience building tool if staff feel isolated and unable to gain the support they need. All case study participants described emersion in a rich professional environment comprising varied, personalized and relevant CPD, as an effective means of building, maintaining and restoring their personal resilience. The significance of high-quality personalized CPD can be viewed as illustrative of the nexus identified in the literature (Beltman, 2015; Day and Gu, 2014; Margolis and Alexandrou, 2014; Ungar, 2012) between teacher resilience and school context. The rich variety of CPD opportunities provides a suitable environment for staff to enhance their skills as an inclusive practitioner in such a way that restores, maintains and builds their resilience. In relation to participants' personal and emotional responsibility to maintain and restore their own resilience, and their social responsibility to consider others' resilience, context also counts. For example, case study participants refer to the culture in their settings (i.e. an appreciation culture, or a culture where open and honest feedback at every level is welcomed). You have seen how important it is from the case studies presented in this chapter for a teacher to value each and every member of the community including themselves. Such valuing requires an understanding of, and provision for, the environment which supports every member's success. The conclusions drawn here point to a symbiosis between the inclusive environment created for children and young people, and, the inclusive supportive environment created for and by staff. This symbiosis echoes Booth and Ainscow's (2011) expansive construction of inclusion, involving both children and adults.

Implications for educators

When reading the implications below, note how each of them locates you the teacher in a context. Consider the response required from both you and the educational setting in which you work to achieve the following.

1. Challenge need not be viewed as a mechanism for depleting staff resilience, but when contextualized in a rich school culture of reflection and reflexive practice, it can be constructed as a driver for increased resilience.
2. Educational settings should reflexively analyse their own behaviours questioning whether attitudes, theories in use, assumptions or habitual actions point to an interventionist paradigm.
3. Educational settings should provide a range of relevant opportunities for staff to embed, reflect upon and reflexively analyse their interventionist approaches to teaching and learning.
4. Through consultation with relevant parties, schools should consider developing an inclusive (Booth and Ainscow, 2011) well-being plan (Hilton, 2018) which actively aims to support and enhance pupil and staff resilience alike. Staff might consider targeting their own well-being through direct engagement with the well-being plan, reflexively analysing whether the tools available to them are efficacious or in need of adjustment.

Finally, focusing on you as an individual in a context, can you list three actions you will try to take to promote the inclusion of pupils with additional needs?

Annotated bibliography

Kroll, L. (2012). *Self study and inquiry into practice: Learning to teach for equality and social justice in the elementary school classroom*. **Abingdon: Routledge.**
Addressing teacher inquiry and reflective practice in a social justice context, this book provides a highly relevant follow-up to this chapter.

Norwich, B. and Jones, J. (2014). *Lesson study: Making a difference to teaching pupils with learning difficulties.* London: Bloomsbury.
This book provides further information about implementing lesson study for the benefit of the child with SEND.

Robinson, D. and Goodey, C. (2017). 'Agency in the darkness: "Fear of the unknown", learning disability and teacher education for inclusion', *International Journal of Inclusive Education*, 22(4), pp. 426–40.
This article provides a thought-provoking analysis of inclusion phobia which is analysed through the lens of preservice teachers' reflections on practicum.

9
The Role of Teachers and Teaching

Sue Soan and Christian Couper

In my day, the term special educational needs had not been created and teachers taught everyone that 'could be' educated in schools. I did not begin to spell or read with any level of competence until I was about twelve, and I had a lisp that meant I couldn't pronounce words clearly and was frequently laughed at by peers. At the age of eleven I failed a national test, at secondary school I was laughed at weekly by my peers when I couldn't read out the French phrases and at sixteen I was told I was too 'thick' to study 'A' levels by a Head teacher. I was a failure … … … except that along this at times devastating journey one or two teachers saw what I could do and not what I couldn't do. They provided me with learning joy and resilience to keep going. I can still name these teachers and recount how they provided me with some feelings of self-worth. For that I have always been thankful. I still doubt myself, think I am a failure, but these experiences gave me values and beliefs that influenced my whole 'worldview' and professional direction. Therefore, can I regret my experiences? Well it meant I have spent my whole career trying to ensure that pupils I worked with never had to experience what I went through … I tried to be a 'Star Thrower'[1] and I am still trying … …

(A seasoned teacher's personal reflection)

Reflexive questions

1. How does this reflection make you feel? Answer this question from both a personal and a professional point of view.
2. Have you or anyone you know had a similar experience and has this impacted on your views and values about teaching pupils with special needs, or gifts and talents?

[1] https://starthrowerfoundation.org/about-starthrower-foundation/the-star-thrower-story/

The role of the teacher

There are as you have read in the previous chapters many different accomplishments that a teacher's role incorporates and many reasons why people decide to become a teacher. We argue here that as teachers your 'Why' is to make a difference, and to have the confidence to make the right decision for each and every pupil. Throughout this book the authors, whether teacher practitioners or education academics, have focused on providing guidance to teachers, to help build their level of resilience, and to become better reflective and reflexive practitioners. Due to the complex, fast-moving global social change described in Chapter 1, it is undoubtable that the teaching role and thus teachers are crucial professionals in the twenty-first century. But managing the constant readjustment of their identity, values and position within their social context is complex and challenging, especially when considering the needs of pupils with a myriad of needs. Indeed, as Gu (2014, p. 4) says, teachers can be the conduit 'bridging the past, the present and the future' during social change, being real and positive change agents.

But this is not easy, as recruitment and retention concerns in countries affirm (Foster, 2018), especially when political, as well as social drivers within education challenge teacher's identities, values and beliefs. As a consequence of such dilemmas this can lead to internal conflict between personal and professional values (Pillen, Den Brock and Beijard, 2013). In many current education systems the performance measurement of pupils (and frequently the teacher through inspection) is a dominant role of the teacher, and this, we suggest, can be a real challenge for teachers who want to put into practice what they consider is best for pupils with special or high ability needs, for example, but conflicts with system requirements. Such constant struggles might lead to teachers becoming risk adverse, disillusioned and compliant (Sachs, 2016; Wood et al., 2020). Add to this professional dilemma recipe a further ingredient of an increase in the marketization of the education system and thus greater service user input (i.e. parents and pupils), teachers, and especially leaders, like the Special Educational Needs Coordinators (SENCos) and Principals, find themselves trying to serve many masters. One response to this changing environment, it can be surmised, has been an increasing range and segregation or integration of provision. These cater for pupils with special educational needs, disabilities and those with high ability (e.g. grammar schools, subject-/talent-focused academies), although this latter provision, it can be argued, is more highly regarded and valued within wider English society. Armstrong and Squires (2012, p. 24) describe this as 'an education system that marks some children out as being different and labels them as having problems defined as SEN'. But is this acceptable practice in the twenty-first century?

Reflective questions

1. Does this level of separation suggest that not all teachers can/need to teach pupils with special educational needs?
2. Does this provide a physical/concrete reason for 'othering' pupils with a special educational need, or a gift or talent in education and/or wider social situations?

Reflexive questions

1. What are your attitudes towards pupils/people with special needs or are able and talented or both?
2. Do you have experiences that have influenced how you feel about this?
3. Do these experiences impact on how you teach pupils with special, able, gifted or talented needs?

The situation, in England, at least becomes even more confusing when reading the National Teachers' Standards (DfE, 2011, updated, 2013, p. 12) which say that all teachers must

> have a clear understanding of the needs of all pupils, including those with special educational needs; those of high ability; those with English as an additional language; those with disabilities; and be able to use and evaluate distinctive teaching approaches to engage and support them.

and the SEND code of practice (DfE and DoH, 2015, p. 99, 6.36) when it says:

> Teachers are responsible and accountable for the progress and development of the pupils in their class, including where pupils access support from teaching assistants or specialist staff.

Balancing such diverse agendas at the national, local and personal level can, we suggest, become difficult for teachers to navigate unless they have the resilience, collaborative support and theoretical underpinnings on which to focus and pursue their professional role to respond to the holistic needs and well-being of the pupil.

It is also important to recognize that teachers will not all have the same personally held views, values and attitudes. Therefore, to meet national agendas, such as inclusive education and valuing diversity, ongoing professional development and opportunities to reflect, to engage with mentoring and coaching, and to have access to supervision are all crucial elements of a professional life, as well as subject knowledge. The following Window on research provides a better understanding of how teacher attitudes might impact on practice working with pupils with special educational needs.

Window on research

Lindblom, A., Dindar, K., Soan, S., Kärnä, E., Roos, C. and Carew, M. T. (2020). 'Predictors and mediators of European student teacher attitudes toward autism spectrum disorder', *Teaching and Teacher Education*, 89(102993), pp. 1–10.

This research sought to find out how teacher training institutions could enhance their provision to more effectively prepare students for teaching pupils with autism spectrum disorders (ASD) in inclusive classrooms in Sweden, Finland and England.

ASD was identified specifically because studies (e.g. Huskin, Reiser-Robbins and Kwon, 2018) had shown that people have more negative attitudes towards those with ASD than people with other disabilities. Although little evidence was found regarding the attitudes of student teachers towards people/pupils with ASD (Barned, Flanagan Knapp and Neuharth-Pritchett, 2011), the literature did show that qualified teacher attitudes were indeed important when determining how well pupils with ASD are included in regular classes (Caplan, Feldman, Eisenhower and Blacher, 2016). In consideration of these findings this study carried out an investigation exploring what predicts student teacher attitudes towards people with ASD.

Data were collected from one university from each of the three countries as representatives for the national teacher education programmes. The sample comprised 704 student teachers (262 in Sweden, 252 in Finland and 191 in England). All were studying teacher education and were aged between 19 and 55. The majority of the students were female (579) (120 males; six did not state their gender).

The study used a cross-sectional design which consisted of a survey which asked participants questions about their attitudes and experiences of people with ASD. All six researchers designed both the survey and the research procedure.

Findings firstly verified that participants' attitudes towards people with ASD were representative of their attitudes towards pupils with ASD specifically. Other data examined explored which predictor(s) uniquely predicts attitudes towards people with ASD and 'whether cognitive beliefs (i.e. stereotypes, concerns) or affect (i.e. intergroup anxiety) toward ASD mediate any identified relationships between the remaining predictors and attitudes toward ASD (i.e.

contact quality, contact quantity, perceptions of course knowledge, perception of social norms)' (Lindblom et al., 2020, p. 6).

Outcomes

The findings from this study suggest that when promoting positive attitudes among student teachers towards pupils with ASD, high-contact quality, reducing affective inter-group anxiety and encouraging positive social norms should be targeted when delivering interventions. As such the study found that having the opportunities to interact with pupils who have ASD is crucial as part of a comprehensive teacher training programme. However, even more important than the quantity of contact is the quality of contact.

The study also found that perceptions of greater knowledge gained through programmes were not associated with attitudes, suggesting that 'perceived increased knowledge does not contribute to positive attitudes toward people with ASD' (ibid., p. 7). This resonated with findings from other studies (e.g. White et al., 2016).

What we can learn

Research such as the one shared above demonstrates how knowledge is not the only factor involved when trying to ensure pupils with additional needs receive a positive and full education. Knowing what and how to teach pupils with ASD or speech and language differences, for example, is important of course. However, a teacher's attitude towards those with differences appears to be a valid element for providing an inclusive learning environment.

Reflective questions

1. Can you remember the first occasion when you saw a pupil with ASD or with a behavioural and emotional need become unresponsive to instructions or become disruptive?
2. How was it resolved?
3. Was it resolved in a pupil-centred manner or not?

Reflexive question

How do you think the pupil's actions and then the teacher's response have influenced your feelings and thoughts about working with pupils with additional needs?

The following case study portrays what a positive attitude towards pupils with, in this case, behavioural and emotional needs can play in a pupil's life in school and future learning experiences.

Case study: A pupil-centred response

Country: South-east England

Age group: 8-year-old pupils

Setting: Mainstream primary school (age 4–11 years)

Participants involved: class peers (32); class teacher; and Colin,[2] the focus pupil

The case study

Colin had not joined the class until two months after the start of the new school year. Prior to joining the school, Colin had attended a PRU (Pupil Referral Unit), but his behaviour had improved so much that the PRU felt he was ready to return to mainstream schooling. The teacher was in her third year of teaching and was enjoying the challenges of working in a socially deprived area. However, the dynamics of the class changed immediately Colin joined the class and he seemed determined to stop everyone else from learning. He looked to receive attention from the teacher at all times and tried to disrupt established peer relationships. Following one particularly challenging day when Colin had been an animal hiding under a group table, making loud noises and upturning chairs and tables, the teacher decided that enough was enough and the situation had to be tackled.

The teacher spent time that evening firstly reflecting on what was really happening for Colin in the classroom and how she was responding to meet his needs. She noted that Colin did not have any friends and that when he 'misbehaved', after asking him to return to his seat or to his task, she mostly ignored him. She began to understand how he might be feeling and decided to change her practice to help him adjust to his new situation.

The teacher adapted her lesson planning and also pupil class responsibilities. Her targets for success were:

a) Colin would begin to establish and develop peer friendships
b) Colin would be able to contribute to the successful running of the class
c) Colin would experience success –in terms of both his behaviour and learning.

The action plan:

[2] Not his real name.

1. The teacher knew that Colin had a great interest in arachnids and so decided the class would commence a project about these creatures. It would be a total curriculum project and the results would be presented at the local County Show by some of the pupils. An arachnid specialist was also invited into the school and Colin was given the responsibility of hosting the guest.
2. Colin was provided with support from his peers in lessons through pair and small group work even if he couldn't manage the whole session.
3. Colin was given permission to get up and walk around the classroom when he needed to and was given a cushion to go and read on when he couldn't cope with class activities. He was also in charge of all crayon sharpening (not pencil) for the class.
4. The teacher would also hold Colin in mind by wearing traffic light cards (red, amber and greed) around her neck. Colin also had these cards on his desk. When he was managing, Colin would place his green card on top; but if he began to become anxious or needed to physically move, he changed the cards to amber or red. As soon as possible the teacher would do the same, showing Colin visually that she had seen his distress and would come and help as soon as she could. The teacher also promoted this form of support with Colin's mother so that this was a consistent approach carried out at home and school.

Outcome

By the end of the academic year Colin was a happy enthusiastic pupil who had positive peer relationships, was able to sit and engage actively in learning for whole lessons and had built productive relationships with the teachers. The teacher was so proud of Colin's achievements and the 'icing on top of the cake' arrived from his new school and his new teacher:

> [*It is clear to us that you must have worked extremely hard to help Colin re-establish himself into mainstream education within an academic year after such previous difficulties which led him to require the support of a PRU.*]

(This is the essence of a letter sent from Colin's new teacher at the beginning of the next academic year in a new school to the teacher in the case study.)

What we can learn

The teacher in this case study showed many elements of professional resilience and evidenced that her underpinning beliefs and values were pupil-centred. Recognizing that the situation in her classroom could not continue, this teacher did not put the emphasis on the pupil to change or seek a diagnosis or further assessments immediately (although in other situations this might have been necessary). Without explicitly knowing it, she used her practice observational skills to recall Colin's behaviours and also took the time to reflect on her own practice and responses to Colin. She saw Colin as a pupil who was probably lonely, feeling an 'outsider' and wanting to be noticed, so instead of putting in behaviour management strategies focused on his problems she decided to change her practice. This shows how reflection, resilience and belief in her professional values helped her channel her teaching skills in a positive direction, supporting rather than disciplining.

And can you guess who was part of the team presenting the project at the County Show? – yes it was Colin ….

Reflective questions

1. Reading through this case study again how many positive elements of the teacher's practice can you note?
2. What would you have done differently (if anything) and would they have all been pupil-centred?

Reflexive questions

1. Thinking back to the day Colin's behaviour caused significant concern for the teacher, how honestly do you think you would have responded?
2. Why do you think this would have been the case?

Not every situation though can be solved so positively and without further input and support from colleagues. It is crucial to recognize that at any stage of a teacher's career a teacher might find balancing 'head and heart' very problematic and could quickly become all-consuming and detrimental to their own well-being. For these reasons we suggest that it is crucial that school communities or groups of teachers establish, support and maintain a shared vision and values that enable them to continue putting the pupils with special, able or dual/multiple exceptionality (DME) at the centre of their practice whilst still completing contractual responsibilities and pupil achievement expectations.

The development of whole school approaches for inclusive practice

In this second part of the chapter we share how critical, reflective and value-based collaborative approaches to teaching can lead to meaningful and permanent positive change for all pupils including those with special and other additional needs (further information can be read in Chapter 8). Ekins (2012) echoes this using a quotation from Reid (2010, p. 136):

> Meaningful change will … only occur when ….'those whose practice is the focus of change are involved in the process of challenging and rethinking the assumptions and theories on which their practice is based. Unless this happens, imposed change in the form of a new 'product' is simply filtered through the lens of established beliefs and practices, and is colonised by that practice. The same things are done but with new labels'.

We are not recommending these approaches per se, but include them to show that these established ways of working model how schools can effectively enable government directives to be achieved alongside philosophies of teaching, using a collective, inclusive and professionally driven approach.

One New Zealand approach

In New Zealand teachers are using, as also seen in Chapter 7, collaborative approaches to support the provision of learning programmes that are requiring greater individualization, are being based in authentic contexts and are able to respond to rapidly changing policy directions from governments. Such practice is not focused on those pupils with additional learning needs alone, but on all pupils – an inclusive approach. For teachers in New Zealand the purpose for school education in this century is to find ways to open up opportunities for [all] their pupils, to help them grow competencies for life, to develop skills and dispositions which will be of worth in their adult life. The following Window on research reports on findings from a thesis regarding key elements that are necessary to underpin this way of working.

Window on research

O'Reilly, N. (2016). *The key components to creating effective collaborative teaching and learning environments.* Thesis Publication University of Canterbury, New Zealand. Available at: https://ir.canterbury.ac.nz/handle/10092/12190

In his thesis findings from a survey of schools in New Zealand, O'Reilly initially identified two fundamental elements that underpin collaborative teaching and learning environments. These were shared beliefs and understandings, and pupil centredness. He elucidates further that a truly pupil-centred approach puts the pupil explicitly at the centre and every teacher (and other professionals) focuses on what makes a difference for the pupil, not easier for the teachers. O'Reilly found that like Hattie's (2016) 'Collective teacher efficacy'[3] (CTE), it was the teacher's role to determine pupil success and achievement by the evidence and engagement of the pupil. He found that teachers who held shared beliefs and understandings ensured they designed programmes together, as early as possible and held close to the school's vision and values. O'Reilly also found that the 'why' and 'how' were defined and understood among collaborative teams and featured in mutually agreed team expectations (MATES). Hence their practice was by design reflecting their school's vision and by evidence having a positive impact on their pupils.

Subsequently, three other elements were found to emerge through O'Reilly's survey of schools. He also found three more features that he felt should be in place for effective pupil learning to take place using CTE. Table 9.1 illustrates these three elements and three features.

Table 9.1 Three sub-elements and features for effective pupil learning using CTE (Hattie, 2016)[1]

Sub-elements	Features
Skill development: In communication, digital and leadership (p. 60)	*Strategies:* Teachers explicitly and consistently enacting strategies for collaboration
Support for staff: CPD, leadership, mindsets, support staff, resourcing (p. 64)	*Structures:* School systems for employment, appraisal and team selection and size
Smart systems: Smart digital goals and systems for meeting pupil's need (p. 73)	*Space flexibility:* For collaborative teaching and learning to take place, flexible spaces are needed

[1] https://visible-learning.org/2018/03/collective-teacher-efficacy-hattie/

Issues for some education systems around the world would not immediately be able to support this approach. However, its purpose here is to show how teacher's values and beliefs can be collaboratively supported and thus might limit possible conflict and stress of individuals, especially when teaching pupils with special, high ability or both.

---

[3] https://visible-learning.org/2018/03/collective-teacher-efficacy-hattie/

One English approach

Similar to the collaborative approach implemented in New Zealand the whole-school inclusive school development initiative *Achievement for All* (AfA), a not-for-profit organization[4] was established with funding from the Department for Education in 2011. Importantly for this discussion and in agreement with O'Reilly's research findings, it is built on the key elements of a shared vision, commitment, collaboration and communication. Its schools programme focuses on four elements: leadership; teaching and learning; structured conversations with parents and carers; and wider outcomes (enjoyment and achievement for all pupils in all areas of school life). An initial pilot study evaluation examining the impact of the programme on the learning achievement of pupils with SEND, entitled 'Achievement for All: effect on SEND pupils' (DfE, 2013), found that children with special educational needs and/or disabilities (SEND) in AfA schools had higher rates of progress than other pupils with SEND. Research is ongoing. It appears that in many areas of their work, collaborative and team working is key. In their recent published manifesto, *Working Together: Every Child Included in Education*, two of their key co-developed priorities are:

1. **Greater focus on teachers as professional learners** through recruitment, retention, and CPD that includes an enhanced understanding of the way disadvantaged and vulnerable children learn.
2. **Reduce children and young people being excluded in education and close the gap for SEND – too often the marginalized and forgotten group.** This includes increasing responsibility for children at risk of exclusion through cross-agency collaboration.[5]

Thus, once again research evidence is that collaborative, pupil-focused and teacher-led approaches can support teachers to successfully maintain and develop their professional role and responsibilities. In both of the examples presented the approaches involve reflective and critical engagement with both professional and personal values and principles which underpin teaching practice.

Reflective questions

1. Reviewing both of the approaches described, what elements do you recognize in your own personal and school's practice?
2. Do you think these working practices will help you develop a greater understanding of how to work effectively with pupils with different learning needs?

[4] https://afaeducation.org/afa-education-trust/
[5] https://afaeducation.org/media/1489/afa-manifesto-final-2205.pdf

3. Do you think a whole school approach to working can help teachers see that they can teach pupils with additional and individual needs in their classroom successfully and happily?

Implications for educators

1. Teaching can be a lonely and challenging profession if collaborative practices are not followed in a school/setting which could lead to greater retention issues.
2. Through collaborative approaches the sharing of ideas and values can provide greater avenues to explore to enable pupils with special educational needs, or those with high ability to be fully included.
3. A pupil-centred approach can ensure every pupil receives an inclusive education.
4. A team approach can enable national professional requirements to be achieved without detriment to the 'heart' element of a teacher's philosophy.
5. Inclusive leadership encompassing a shared vision, commitment, collaboration and communication can really support the teacher's role and responsibility.

Conclusion: A future view

Wouldn't it be amazing if in the near future, we can all accept that everyone is different and that this is not seen as a problem by societies? Armstrong and Squires (2012, p. 24) nearly a decade ago wrote about a different world where:

> We do not necessarily need to conceptualise special educational needs [or other different needs] but could simply recognise individual differences and patterns of strengths as well as weaknesses .... It is a world in which teachers are allowed to develop skills and expertise in supporting all pupils. In this world, professionals work together to help the teacher become more effective, whereas, in the real one, there is a temptation to see professionals that are 'experts' who 'treat' 'conditions'.

Concluding comments

We hope that this book helps you see how significant your role is and why every teacher needs to know about all about diverse learning needs. Without understanding 'Why', teachers cannot effectively answer the questions 'how', 'what' and for 'whom' and therefore are unable to see their role and responsibilities in providing every pupil with the education they deserve. Are you a teacher who can give pupils with complex challenges and needs the joy of learning, resilience and enable school to be a happy place?

> *It would be great to work in a system where labels for difference were not the method for getting appropriate resource allocations. If we were to approach any school group as a collection of diverse individuals, who are learning how to flourish together, could we do away with the prejudice and low aspirations?*

> (Christian Couper)

Reflect

Annotated bibliography

Armstrong, D. and Squires, G. (eds.) (2012). *Contemporary issues in special educational needs: Considering the whole child.* **Maidenhead: OUP.**
This book draws together the many voices of people engaged actively in special educational needs and disability research and practice. By doing this it provides a challenging commentary on current-day complex issues for those working with and interested in the field of special educational needs. The different perspectives offered provide the reader with much to consider and ponder.

Booth, T. and Ainscow, M. (2011). *Index for inclusion: Developing learning and participation in schools.* **Bristol: Centre for Studies on Inclusive Education.**
This third edition of the Index is a school self-evaluation and improvement resource which is values-based and promotes inclusive education as a notion built on equality and human rights. A new school curriculum is outlined in detail in this edition and this can be adopted for use in any part of the world.

Montgomery, D. (ed.) (2009). *Able, gifted and talented underachievers.* **2nd edn. Chichester: John Wiley and Sons Ltd.**
In this book, Montgomery and others explicitly show that our higher-ability or talented pupils frequently can experience the same difficulties as those identified as experiencing special educational needs. Issues relating to teaching these individuals can be similar as well. One comment in the conclusions could echo the many discussions housed within this volume:

> These three case studies show how schools that have high quality leadership and good teachers working as a team, knowledgeable about teaching and learning effectively can make a difference.

> (ibid., p. 340)

References

Chapter 1 Setting the Context

Betts, G. and Neihart, M. (1988). 'Profiles of the gifted and talented', *Gifted Child Quarterly*, Milton Keynes: NAGC (now Potential Plus UK). Available at: https://www.potentialplusuk.org/

Bronfenbrenner, U. (1989). 'Ecological systems theory', in Vasta, R. (ed.) *Annals of child development* (Vol. 6). Boston, MA: JAI Press, pp. 187–249.

DfE (2011). *Support and aspiration: A new approach to special educational needs and disability: A consultation.* Norwich: TSO.

Department for Education and Department of Health (2014). *Special educational needs code of practice: 0–25.* London: DfE.

Department for Education and Department of Health (January 2015). *Special educational needs code of practice: 0–25.* London: DfE.

Department for Education and Science (DES) (1981). *Education Act 1981.* London: HMSO.

Department for Education and Skills (DfES) (2001). *Special educational needs code of practice.* London: DfES.

HMSO (1978). *Warnock Report: Special Educational Needs, Report of the Committee of Enquiry into the Education of Handicapped Children and Young People.* London: HMSO.

Ofsted (2019). *The Ofsted Inspection Framework.* May. Available at: https://assets.publishing.service.gov.uk/government/uploads/system/uploads/attachment_data/file/801429/Education_inspection_framework.pdf

Rose, R., Shevlin, M., Winter, E. and O'Raw, P. (2015). *Project IRIS – Inclusive research in Irish Schools. A longitudinal study of the experiences of and outcomes for children with special educational needs (SEN) in Irish Schools.* National Council for Special Education.

Schwartz, J., Hatfield, S., Jones, R. and Anderson, S. (2019). *What is the future of work?* Available at: https://www2.deloitte.com/content/dam/Deloitte/nl/Documents/humancapital/deloitte-nl-hc-what-is-the-future-of-work.pdf

UNESCO (2000). *The Dakar Framework for Action: Education for All: Meeting our collective commitments.* France: UNESCO. Available at: https://resourcecentre.savethechildren.net/node/2023/pdf/2023.pdf

Chapter 2 The Professional Self and Diverse Learning Needs

Black, A., Lawson, H. and Norwich, B. (2019). 'Lesson plan for diversity', *Journal of Research in Special Educational Needs*, 19(2), pp. 115–25. doi:10.1111/1471-3802.12433.

Bronfenbrenner, U. (1989). 'Ecological systems theory', in Vasta, R. (ed.) *Annals of child development* (Vol. 6). Boston, MA: JAI Press, pp. 187–249.

Carter, B. B. and Spencer, V. G. (2006). 'The fear factor: And students with disabilities', *International Journal of Special Education*, 21, pp. 11–23.

Elliot, J. (1991). *Action research for educational change*. Buckingham: Open University Press.

Erikson, E. H. (1950). *Childhood and society*. New York: W. W. Norton.

European Agency for Development in Special Education (EADSNE) (2012). 'Teacher education for inclusion: Profile of inclusive teachers'. Available at: https://www.european-agency.org/sites/default/files/Profile-of-Inclusive-Teachers.pdf

Fletcher-Watson, S. and Happé, F. (2019). *Autism: A new introduction to psychological theory and current debate*. London: Routledge.

Lundy, L. (2007). '"Voice" is not enough: Conceptualising Article 12 of the United Nations Convention on the Rights of the Child', *British Educational Research Journal*, 33(6), pp. 927–42. doi:10.1080/01411920701657033.

Lynam, A. M., McConnell, B. and Mc Guckin, C. (2018). *BeSAD (Bereavement, Separation, and Divorce): The response of pre-service teachers to pupil well- being. A report for the Standing Conference on Teacher Education North and South (SCoTENS)*. Armagh, Northern Ireland: The Centre for Cross Border Studies. ISBN: 978-1-9997543-2-7: Available at: https://www.tcd.ie/Education/news/scotens-conference2018/BeSAD-Report.pdf

Marshall, K. (2016). 'Rethinking differentiation: Using teachers' time most effectively', *Phi Delta Kappan*, 98(1), pp. 8–13. doi:10.1177/0031721716666046.

Mc Guckin, C. and Minton, S. (2014). 'From theory to practice: Two ecosystemic approaches and their applications to understanding school bullying', *Australian Journal of Guidance and Counselling*, 24(1), 36–48. doi:10.1017/jgc.2013.10.

Montgomery, D. (2015). *Teaching gifted children with special educational needs: Supporting dual and multiple exceptionality*. London: Routledge.

Norwich, B. and Kelly, N. (2004). 'Pupils' views on inclusion: Moderate learning difficulties and bullying in mainstream and special schools', *British Educational Research Journal*, 30(1), pp. 43–65. doi:10.1080/01411920310001629965..

O'Brien, A. M. and Mc Guckin, C. (2014). 'Grieving students: The response and support of Irish schools', *Trinity College Dublin Journal of Postgraduate Research*, 13, pp. 159–76. ISSN: 2009–4787: Available at: http://hdl.handle.net/2262/72482.

O'Síoráin, C. (2017). *An inquiry into the literacy practices of pupils with autism in mainstream primary settings in the Republic of Ireland* (Unpublished doctoral thesis). Trinity College Dublin, Ireland.

O'Síoráin, C., Shevlin, M. and Mc Guckin, C. (2018). 'Discovering gems: Authentic listening to the "voice" of experience in teaching pupils with autism', in Mooney, B. (ed.) *Education matters: Ireland's yearbook of education*. Dublin, Ireland: Education Matters, pp. 171–5. Available at: https://educationmatters.ie/irelands-yearbook-of-education-2018-2019/

Organisation for Economic Co-operation and Development (OECD) (2010). *Education at a glance 2010: OECD indicators*. Paris: OECD. Available at: http://www.oecd.org/education/skills-beyond-school/educationataglance2010oecdindicators.htm

Paterson, D. (2007). 'Teachers' in-flight thinking in inclusive classrooms', *Journal of Learning Disabilities*, 40(5), pp. 427–35. doi:10.1177/00222194070400050601.

Preece, D. and Howley, M. (2018). 'An approach to supporting young people with autism spectrum disorder and high anxiety to reengage with formal education – The impact on young people and their families', *International Journal of Adolescence and Youth*, 23(4), 468–81. doi:10.1080/02673843.2018.1433695.

Purdy, N. and Mc Guckin, C. (2014). 'Disablist bullying: What student teachers in Northern Ireland and the Republic of Ireland don't know and the implications for teacher education', *European Journal of Special Needs Education*, 29(4), pp. 446–56. doi:10.1080/08856257.2014.952914.

Quirke, M. and McCarthy, P. (2020). *A conceptual framework of Universal Design for Learning (UDL) for the Irish Further Education and Training Sector: 'Where Inclusion is Everyone's Business'*. Dublin, Ireland: SOLAS.

Rix, J. (2015). *Must inclusion be special: Rethinking educational support within a community of provision*. London: Routledge.

Robinson, D. (2017). 'Effective inclusive teacher education for special educational needs and disabilities: Some more thoughts on the way forward', *Teaching and Teacher Education*, 61, pp. 164–78. doi:10.1016/j.tate.2016.09.007.

Rose, R., Shevlin, M., Winter, E. and O'Raw, P. (2015). *Project IRIS–Inclusive Research in Irish Schools. A longitudinal study of the experiences of and outcomes for children with special educational needs (SEN) in Irish Schools*. National Council for Special Education.

Safi, O. (2014, November 6). *The disease of being busy*. [Blog post]. Available at: https://onbeing.org/blog/the-disease-of-being-busy/

Salokangas, M. and Ainscow, M. (2018). *Inside the autonomous school – Making sense of a global educational trend*. Oxon: Routledge.

Smit, B. and Scherman, V. (2016). 'A case for relational leadership and an ethics of care for counteracting bullying at schools', *South African Journal of Education*, 36(4), pp. 1–9. doi:10.15700/saje.v36n4a1312.

Soini, T., Pietarinen, J., Pyhältö, K., Jindal-Snape, D. and Kontu, E. (2019). 'Special education teachers' experienced burnout and perceived fit with the professional community: A 5-year follow-up study', *British Educational Research Journal*, 45(3), pp. 622–39. doi:10.1002/berj.3516.

United Nations Educational Scientific and Cultural Organisation (UNESCO) (1994). *The Salamanca statement on principles, policy and practice in special needs education*. Paris, France: UNESCO.

United Nations (UN) General Assembly (2000). 'United Nations Millenium Declaration', *United Nations(UN)General Assembly*. Available at: https://doi.org/ http://www.undp.org/content/undp/en/home/mdgoverview.html

United Nations (UN) General Assembly (2015). *Transforming our world: The 2030 agenda for sustainable development. United Nations(UN)General Assembly*. Available at: https://doi.org/10.1007/s13398-014-0173-7.2

Warnock, M. (1978). *Special educational needs: Report of the Committee of Enquiry into the education of handicapped children and young people*. London: Her Majesty's Stationery Office.

Warnock, M. and Brahms, N. (2010) *Special educational needs: A new look* Terzi, L. (ed.). 2nd edn. London: Continuum.

Woods, P. A. and Roberts, A. (2018). *Collaborative school leadership: A critical guide*. London: Sage.

Chapter 3 Health and Well-Being

ACT (2009). *A guide to the development of children's palliative care services.* 3rd edn. Bristol: ACT. Available at: https://edisciplinas.usp.br/pluginfile.php/4282446/mod_ folder/content/0/ACT.%20A%20Guide%20to%20the%20Development%20%20 of%20Childrens%20Palliative%20Care%20Services.pdf?forcedownload=1

Anderson, M. and Cardoza, K. (2016). *Mental health in schools: A hidden crisis affecting millions of students*, NPR.org, 31 August, *Part One in an NPR Ed series on mental health in schools.*

Bainbridge, A., Reid, H. and Del Negro, G. (2019). 'Towards a virtuosity of school leadership: Clinical support and supervision as professional learning', *Professional Development in Education.* doi:10.1080/19415257.2019.1700152.

Department for Education (2015). *Supporting pupils at school with medical conditions: statutory guidance for governing bodies of maintained schools and proprietors of academies in England.* London: DfE.

Department for Education and Department of Health (2014). *Special educational needs and disability code of practice: 0–25.* London: DfE.

Department for Education and Department of Health (2015). *Special educational needs and disability code of practice: 0–25.* London: DfE.

Department of Health (2014). *Closing the gap: Priorities for essential change in mental health.* London: DoH.

Ekins, A. (2017) *Reconsidering inclusion: Sustaining and building inclusive practices in schools.* London: Routledge.

Hall, S., Fildes, J., Perrens, B., Plummer, J., Carlisle, E., Cockayne, N. and Werner-Seidler, A. (2019). 'Can we talk? Seven year youth mental health report – 2012–2018', Mission Australia: Sydney, NSW.

House of Commons (2019). 'Children and young people's mental health- policy, services, funding and education', Briefing paper No. 07196. London: HoC.

Internet 1. https://www.leedsbeckett.ac.uk/carnegie-school-of-education/national-hubfor-supervision-in-education/

Jerrim, J., Taylor, H., Sims, S. and Allen, R. (2020). 'Has the mental health and wellbeing of teachers in England declined over time? New evidence from three datasets'. Available at: https://johnjerrim.files.wordpress.com/2020/01/jerrim-working_paper_21_01_2020_clean.pdf

National Audit Office (2019). *Support for pupils with special educational needs and disabilities in England*, DfE. Available at: https://www.nao.org.uk/report/support-for-pupils-with-special-educational-needs-and-disabilities/

Reid, H. and Soan, S. (2015). *Supervision: A business and community service for colleagues in schools*. Evaluation Report, Canterbury Christ Church University: Faculty of Education.

Reid, H. and Soan, S. (2018). 'Providing support to senior managers in schools via 'clinical' supervision: A restorative and purposeful professional and personal space', *Professional Development in Education*, 45(1), 59–72. doi:10.1080/19415257.2018.1427132.

Robinson, S. and Summers, K. (2012). 'An evaluation of the educational support for teachers who teach children with life-limiting illness in schools', *Pastoral Care in Education*, 30(3), 191–207. doi: 10.1080/02643944.2012.671341

Välimaa, R., Kannas, L., Lahtinen, E., Peltonen, H., Tynjälä, J. and Villberg, J. (2007). 'Finland: Innovative health education curriculum and other investments for promoting mental health and social cohesion among children and young people'. Available at: http://www.euro.who.int/__data/assets/pdf_file/0007/74761/Hbsc_Forum_2007_Finland.pdf

Worth, J., Lynch, S., Hillary, J., Rennie, C. and Andrade, J. (2018). *Teacher workforce dynamics in England*. Slough: NFER.

Chapter 4 The Learning Environment

Austin, R. (ed.) (2007). *Letting the outside in – Developing teaching and learning beyond the early years classroom*. Stoke on Trent: Trentham Books Limited.

Australian Institute for Teaching and School Leadership Limited (aitsl) (2011). *Australian professional standards for teachers*. Available at: https://www.aitsl.edu.au/docs/default-source/national-policy-framework/australian-professional-standards-for-teachers.pdf?sfvrsn=5800f33c_64

Bronfenbrenner, U. (1979). *The ecology of human development: Experiments by nature and design*. Cambridge, MA: Harvard University Press.

Buckingham, D. (2000). *After the death of childhood: Growing up in the age of electronic media*. Cambridge: Polity Press.

Byers, T., Imms, W. and Hartnell-Young, E. (2018). 'Evaluating teacher and student spatial transition from a traditional classroom to an innovative learning environment', *Studies in Educational Evaluation*, 58, pp. 156–66.

Couper, L. and Sutherland, D. (2019). *Learning and connecting in school playgrounds: Using the playground as a curriculum resource*. Abingdon: Routledge.

Davies, R. and Hamilton, P. (2018). 'Assessing learning in the early years' outdoor classroom: Examining challenges in practice', *Education 3–13*, 46(1), pp. 117–29.

Department for Education (DfE) (2011). *Teachers' standards*. Available at: https://www.gov.uk/government/publications/teachers-standards.

Department for Education and Department of Health (2014). *Special educational needs and disability code of practice: 0–25*. London: DfE.

Department for Education and Department of Health (2015). *Special educational needs and disability code of practice: 0–25*. London: DfE.

Department for Education and Department of Health (DfE and DoH). (2015). *Special educational needs and disability code of practice: 0 to 25 years*. London: Crown Copyright.

Department of Health (DoH) (2009). *Valuing employment now: Real jobs for people with learning disabilities*. London: Department of Health.

Dillenburger, K., Matuska, E., De Bruijn, M. and Rüdiger Röttgers, H. (2019). *Job coaches for adults with disabilities: A practical guide*. London: Jessica Kingsley Publishers.

Elson, N. (2011). 'Which way next? What is the real choice for students leaving a special school?', *Support for Learning*, 26(4), pp. 152–9.

Etherington, N. (2012). *Gardening for children with Autism spectrum disorders and special educational needs*. London: Jessica Kingsley Publishers.

Hall, E. and Wilton, R. (2011). 'Alternative spaces of 'work' and inclusion for disabled people', *Disability & Society*, 26(7), pp. 867–80.

Hughes, M. and Pollard, A. (2006). 'Home-school knowledge exchange in context', *Educational Review*, 58(4), pp. 385–95.

Lambe, S., Russell, A., Butler, C., Fletcher, S., Ashwin, C. and Brosnan, M. (2019). 'Autism and the transition to university from the student perspective', *Autism*, 23(6): 1531–41. doi:10.1177/1362361318803935

Lowrey, K. A., Hollingshead, A. and Howery, K. A. (2017). 'Closer look: Examining teachers' language around UDL, inclusive classrooms, and intellectual disability', *Intellectual and Developmental Disabilities*, 55(1), pp. 15–24. doi:10.1352/1934-9556-55.1.15

Maciver, T. (2012). 'Developing practice and delivering a forest school programme for children identified as gifted and talented', in Knight, S. (ed.) *Forest school for all*. London: Sage, pp. 41–53.

Malone, K. and Waite, S. (2016). 'Student outcomes and natural schooling: Pathways to evidence and impact report 2016', Plymouth: Plymouth University. Available at: http://www.plymouth.ac.uk/research/oelres-net

Maslow, A. H. (1954). *Motivation and personality*. New York: Harper and Row.

Moll, L. and Greenberg, J. (1990). 'Creating zones of possibilities: Combining social contexts for instruction', in Moll, L. (ed.) *Vygotsky and education: Instructional implications and applications of socio-historical psychology*. Cambridge: Cambridge University Press.

Mulcahy, D. (2015). 'Re/assembling spaces of learning in victorian government schools: Policy enactments, pedagogic encounters and micropolitics', *Discourse: Studies in the Cultural Politics of Education*, 36(4), pp. 500–14.

Neenan, C. and Knight, S. (2012). ' Supporting emotional and social development in forest school with adolescents', in Knight, S. (ed.) *Forest school for all*. London: Sage, pp. 67–79.

Oblinger, D. (2006). *Learning spaces*. Louisville, CO: Educause.

Skellern, J. and Astbury, G. (2012). 'Gaining employment: The experience of students at a further education college for individuals with learning disabilities', *British Journal of Learning Disabilities*, 42, pp. 60–7.

Sutherland, D. and Gosteva, A. (2019). 'Playgrounds for learning, communicating and playing', in Couper and Sutherland (eds.) *Learning and connecting in school playgrounds: Using the playground as a curriculum resource*. Abingdon: Routledge.

understood.org (2019). *Universal design for learning*. Available at: https://www. understood.org/en/school-learning/for-educators/universal-design-for-learning/ understanding-universal-design-for-learning#item0

United Nations Educational, Scientific and Cultural Organization (2019a). 'United Nations Sustainable Development Goals Knowledge Platform'. Available at: https:// sustainabledevelopment.un.org/?menu=1300

United Nations Educational, Scientific and Cultural Organization (UNESCO) (2019b). *Meeting Commitments: Are Countries on Track to Achieve SDG 4?* Paris, Global Education Monitoring Report UNESCO.

United Nations International Children's Emergency Fund Jamaica (2016). *Deaf Can! Coffee: empowered youths brewing a thriving business*. Available at: https://blogs. unicef.org/jamaica/deaf-can-coffee/

Vincent, S. (1999). *The multigrade classroom: A resource handbook for small, rural schools. Book 2: Classroom organization*. Portland, OR: Northwest Regional Educational Lab (Rural Education Program).

Woolner, P., McCarter, S., Wall, K. and Higgins, S. (2012). 'Changed learning through changed space. When can a participatory approach to the learning environment challenge perceptions and alter practice?' *Improving Schools*, 15(1), pp. 45–60.

Chapter 5 Technology

Adam, T. and Tatnall, A. (2017). 'The value of using ICT in the education of school students with learning difficulties', *Education and Information Technologies*, 22, pp. 2711–26. doi: 10.1007/s10639-017-9605-2

Ainscow, M. and César, M. (2006). 'Inclusive education ten years after Salamanca: Setting the agenda', *European Journal of Psychology of Education*, 21(3), pp. 231–8.

Alper, S. and Raharinirina, S. (2006). 'Assistive technology for individuals with disabilities: A review and synthesis of the literature', *Journal of Special Education Technology*, 21(2), pp. 47–64.

Armstrong, F., Armstrong, D. and Barton, L. (2016). *Inclusive education: Policy, contexts and comparative perspectives*. London: Routledge.

Biesta, G. (2015). 'What is education for? On good education, teacher judgement, and educational professionalism', *European Journal of Education*, 50(1), pp. 75–87.

Billinghurst, M. and Duenser, A. (2012). 'Augmented reality in the classroom', *Computer*, 45(7), pp. 56–63.

Bloomberg, K. and Johnson, H. (1990). 'A statewide demographic survey of people with severe communication impairments', *Augmentative and Alternative Communication*, 6(1), pp. 50–60.

Bondy, A. S. and Frost, L. A. (1994). 'The picture exchange communication system', *Focus on Autistic Behavior*, 9(3), pp. 1–19. doi:10.1177/108835769400900301

Bondy, A. S. and Frost, L. A. (2001). 'The picture exchange communication system', *Behavior Modification*, 25, pp. 725–44. doi:10.1177/014544550125500

Borg, J., Larsson, S. and Östergren, P. O. (2011). 'The right to assistive technology: For whom, for what, and by whom?' *Disability & Society*, 26(2), pp. 151–67.

Chinn, S. (2018). *Maths learning difficulties, dyslexia and dyscalculia*. 2nd edn. London: Jessica Kingsley.

Costantino, M. A. and Bonati, M. (2014). 'A scoping review of interventions to supplement spoken communication for children with limited speech or language skills', *PloS One*, 9(3), p. e90744.

Deuchar, M. (2013). *British sign language*. London: Routledge.

Devarakonda, C. (2012). *Diversity and inclusion in early childhood: An introduction*. London: Sage.

DFE and DoH (2015). 'SEN and disability code of practice 0 to 25 years', DFE: London. Available at: https://assets.publishing.service.gov.uk/government/uploads/system/uploads/attachment_data/file/398815/SEND_Code_of_Practice_January_2015.pdf

Dillenbourg, P. and Evans, M. (2011). 'Interactive tabletops in education', *International Journal of Computer-Supported Collaborative Learning*, 6(4), pp. 491–514.

Durkin, K., Boyle, J., Hunter, S. and Conti-Ramsden, G. (2015). 'Video games for children and adolescents with special educational needs', *Zeitschrift Für Psychologie*, 221(2), pp. 79–89.

Edyburn, D. L., Kavita, R. and Hariharan, P. (2017). 'Technological practices supporting diverse students in inclusive settings', in Hughes, M. T. and Talbott, E. (eds.) *The Wiley handbook of diversity in special education*. Chichester: John Wiley and Sons, pp. 357–78.

Egan, K. (1978). 'What is curriculum?' *Curriculum Inquiry*, 8(1), pp. 65–72.

Equality Act (2010). Available at: www.legislation.gov.uk/ukpga/2010/15/pdfs/ukpga_20100015_en.pdf

Ethnologue. (2020). 'Ethnologue'. Available at: https://www.ethnologue.com/subgroups/sign-language

Hattie, J. (2009). *Visible learning: A synthesis of over 800 meta-analyses relating to achievement*. London: Routledge.

Hayhoe, S. (2014). 'The need for inclusive accessible technologies for students with disabilities and learning difficulties', in Burke, L. (ed.) *Learning in a digitalized* age: *Plugged in, turned on, totally engaged?*. Melton, UK: John Catt Educational Publishing, pp. 257–74.

Hayhoe, S. (2015). 'A pedagogical evaluation of accessible settings in Google's Android and Apple's IoS mobile operating systems and native apps using the SAMR model of educational technology and an educational model of technical captial'. Presentation at *INTED2015 Proceedings*, Spain, pp. 2220–8. IATED. Available at: https://library.iated.org/view/HAYHOE2015APE

Hayhoe, S., Roger, K., Eldritch-Böersen, S. and Kelland, L. (2015). 'Developing inclusive technical capital beyond the disabled students' allowance in England', *Social Inclusion*, 3(6), pp. 29–41.

Hehir, T., Grindal, T., Freeman, B., Lamoreau, R., Borquaye, Y. and Burke, S. (2016). 'A summary of the evidence on inclusive education', ABT Associates. Available at: http://alana.org.br/wp-content/uploads/2016/12/A_Summary_of_the_evidence_on_inclusive_education.pdf

Henwood, K. S., Chou, S. and Browne, K. D. (2015). 'A systematic review and meta-analysis on the effectiveness of CBT informed anger management', *Aggression and Violent Behavior*, 25, pp. 280–92.

Hillman, H. and Chapman, C. (2018). 'Biofeedback and anger management: A literature review', *NeuroRegulation*, 5(1), p. 43.

Housand, B. and Housand, A. (2012). 'The role of technology in gifted students' motivation', *Psychology in the Schools*, 49(7), pp. 706–15.

Illeris, K. (2014). 'Transformative learning and identity', *Journal of Transformative Education*, 12(2), pp. 148–63.

Kahn, J., Ducharme, P., Rotenberg, A. and Gonzalez-Heydrich, A. (2013). '"RAGE-control": A game to build emotional strength', *Games for Health: Research, Development, and Clinical Applications*, 2(1), pp. 53–7.

Lancioni, G. E., O'Reilly, M. F., Cuvo, A. J., Singh, N. N., Sigafoos, J. and Didden, R. (2007). 'PECS and VOCAs to enable students with developmental disabilities to make requests: An overview of the literature', *Research in Developmental Disabilities*, 28(5), pp. 468–88. doi:10.1016/j.ridd.2006.06.003

Law, J., Plunkett, C. and Stringer, H. (2012). 'Communication interventions and their impact on behaviour in the young child: A systematic review', *Child Language Teaching and Therapy*, 28(1), pp. 7–23.

Light, J. and McNaughton, D. (2012). 'Supporting the communication, language, and literacy development of children with complex communication needs: State of the science and future research priorities', *Assistive Technology*, 24(1), pp. 34–44.

Mesibov, G. and Shea, V. (2010). 'The TEACCH program in the era of evidence-based practice', *Journal of Autism and Developmental Disorders*, 40(5), pp. 570–9.

Mitchell, D. (2007). *What really works in special and inclusive education: Using evidence-based teaching strategies*. London: Routledge.

Montgomery, D. (2015). *Teaching gifted children with special educational needs: Supporting dual and multiple exceptionality*. London: Routledge.

Moore, A. and Lynch, H. (2015). 'Accessibility and usability of playground environments for children under 12: A scoping review', *Scandinavian Journal of Occupational Therapy*, 22(5), pp. 331–44.

Müller-Tomfelde, C. (ed.) (2010). *Tabletops-horizontal interactive displays*. London: Springer.

Northcote, M., Mildenhall, P., Marshall, L. and Swan, P. (2010). 'Interactive whiteboards: Interactive or just whiteboards?' *Australasian Journal of Educational Technology*, 26(4), pp. 494–510.

Norton, P. and Hathaway, D. (2010). 'Video production as an instructional strategy: Content learning and teacher practice', *Contemporary Issues in Technology and Teacher Education*, 10(1), pp. 145–66.

OHCHR (2016). 'Report of the inquiry concerning the United Kingdom of Great Britain and Northern Ireland carried out by the Committee under Article 6 of the Optional Protocol to the Convention', United Nations Committee on the Rights of Persons with Disabilities. United Nations. Available at: https://www.ohchr.org/EN/HRBodies/CRPD/Pages/InquiryProcedure.aspx

Power, M. and Dalgleish, T. (2016). *Cognition and emotion: From order to disorder*. 3rd edn. New York: Psychology Press.

Riordan, J. P. (2020). 'A method and framework for video-based pedagogy analysis', *Research in Science and Technological Education*. doi:10.1080/02635143.2020.1776243

Robacker, C., Rivera, C. and Warren, S. (2016). 'A token economy made easy through ClassDojo', *Intervention in School and Clinic*, 52(1), pp. 39–43.

Siegle, D. (2017). 'Technology: Encouraging creativity and problem solving through coding', *Gifted Child Today*, 40(2), pp. 117–23.

Siegle, D. (2015). 'Using QR codes to differentiate learning for gifted and talented students', *Gifted Child Today*, 38(1), pp. 63–6.

Sigafoos, J. and Lacono, T. (1993). 'Selecting augmentative communication devices for persons with severe disabilities: Some factors for educational teams to consider', *Australia and New Zealand Journal of Developmental Disabilities*, 18(3), pp. 133–46.

Slough, S. and Connell, M. (2006). 'Defining technogogy and its natural corollary, Technogogical Content Knowledge (TCK)', Association for the Advancement of Computing in Education, March.

Sprague, D. R. and Shaklee, B. (2015). 'Differentiating through technology for gifted students', in *Cases on Instructional Technology in Gifted and Talented Education*. IGI Global, pp. 269–86. Available at: https://doi.org/10.4018/978-1-4666-6489-0.ch013

Swan, B., Coulombe-Quach, X.-L., Huang, A., Godek, J., Becker, D. and Zhou, Y. (2015). 'Meeting the needs of gifted and talented students: Case study of a virtual learning lab in a rural middle school', *Journal of Advanced Academics*, 26(4), pp. 294–319.

Thaler, L. and Goodale, M. A. (2016). 'Echolocation in humans: an overview', *Wiley Interdisciplinary Reviews: Cognitive Science*, 7(6): 382–93.

Todis, B. (1996). 'Tools for the task? Perspectives on assistive technology in educational settings', *Journal of Special Education Technology*, 13(2), pp. 49–61.

van der Meer, L., Sigafoos, J., O'Reilly, M. and Lancioni, G. (2011). 'Assessing preferences for AAC options in communication interventions for individuals with developmental disabilities: A review of the literature', *Research in Developmental Disabilities*, 32(5), pp. 1422–31.

World Health Organisation (WHO) (2018). *Deafness prevention*. Available at: https://www.who.int/deafness/estimates/en/

World Health Organisation (WHO) (2019). *Blindness and visual impairment*, Available at: https://www.who.int/health-topics/blindness-and-vision-loss#tab=tab_1

Wright, J., Sheehy, K., Parsons, S. and Abbott, C. (2011). *Guidelines for research into the effectiveness of assistive technologies (AT)*. London: Kings College London/De Montford University Leicester.

Zabala, J. (2005). 'Ready, SETT, Go! Getting started with the SETT framework', *Closing the Gap*, 23(6), pp. 1–3.

Chapter 6 Empowerment – The Power of Observation and Listening

Alderson, P. (2000). 'School students' views on school councils and daily life at school', *Children & Society*, 14(2), pp. 121–34.

Astington, J. W. and Edward, M. J. (2010). 'The development of theory of mind in early childhood', *Encyclopedia on Early Childhood Development*, 2010, pp. 1–6.

Baron-Cohen, S. E., Tager-Flusberg, H. E. and Cohen, D. J. (1994). 'Understanding other minds: Perspectives from autism', Most of the chapters in this book were presented in draft form at a workshop in Seattle, April 1991. Oxford: Oxford University Press.

Bourdieu, P. (1986). 'The forms of capital', in Richardson, J. (ed.) *Handbook of theory and research for the sociology of education*. New York: Greenwood, pp. 241–58.

Brookfield, S. (1990). *Using critical incidents to explore learners' assumptions. Fostering critical reflection in adulthood: A guide to transformative and emancipatory learning*. San Francisco, CA: Jossey-Bass Publishers, pp. 177–93.

Clark, A. and Moss, P. (2011). *Listening to young children: The mosaic approach*. London: Jessica Kingsley Publishers.

Clark, C., Dyson, A., Millward, A. and Robson, S. (1999). 'Theories of inclusion, theories of schools: Deconstructing and reconstructing the 'inclusive school', *British Educational Research Journal*, 25(2), pp. 157–77.

Cox, S. and Robinson-Pant, A. (2006). 'Enhancing participation in primary school and class councils through visual communication', *Cambridge Journal of Education*, 36(4), pp. 515–32.

Department for Education and Department of Health (DfE and DoH) (2015). *Special educational needs and disability code of practice: 0 to 25 years*. London: Department for Education.

Ferguson, P. M. and Asch, A. (1989). 'Lessons from life: Personal and parental perspectives on school, childhood, and disability', in Biklen, D. P., Ferguson, D. L. and Ford, A. (eds.) *Schooling and disability: Eighty-eighth yearbook of the National Society for the Study of Education*, Part II. Chicago: National Society for the Study of Education, pp. 108–40.

Fielding, M. (2001). 'Students as radical agents of change', *Journal of Educational Change*, 2(2), pp. 123–41.

Geake, J. G. and Gross, M. U. (2008). 'Teachers' negative affect toward academically gifted students: An evolutionary psychological study', *Gifted Child Quarterly*, 52(3), pp. 217–31.

Hammarberg, T. (1990). 'The UN convention on the rights of the child–and how to make it work', *Human Rights Quarterly*, 12(1), pp. 97–105.

Hart, R. A. (1992). 'Children's participation: From tokenism to citizenship' (No. inness92/6). Florence: UNICEF Innocenti Centre.

Hess, R., Molina, A. M. and Kozleski, E. B. (2006). 'Until somebody hears me: Parent voice and advocacy in special educational decision making', *British Journal of Special Education*, 33(3): 148–57. doi:10.1111/j.1467-8578.2006.00430.x

James, A., Jenks, C. and Prout, A. (1998). *Theorizing childhood*. Cambridge: Polity Press.

Koshy, V., Smith, C. P. and Brown, J. (2017). 'Parenting "gifted and talented" children in urban areas: Parents' voices', *Gifted Education International*, 33(1), pp. 3–17.

Long, L., McPhillips, T., Shevlin, M. and Smith, R. (2012). 'Utilising creative methodologies to elicit the views of young learners with additional needs in literacy', *Support for Learning*, 27(1), pp. 20–8.

Lundy, L. (2018). 'In defence of tokenism? Implementing children's right to participate in collective decision-making', *Childhood*, 25(3), pp. 340–54.

Marrable, T. (2014). 'Emotion in responses to the child with "additional needs"', *Child & Family Social Work*, 19(4), pp. 401–10.

Maslow, A. H. (1954). *Motivation and personality*. New York: Harper and Row.

Messiou, K. (2012). 'Collaborating with children in exploring marginalisation: An approach to inclusive education', *International Journal of Inclusive Education*, 16(12), pp. 1311–22.

Messiou, K. (2019). 'Understanding marginalisation through dialogue: A strategy for promoting the inclusion of all students in schools', *Educational Review*, 71(3), pp. 306–17.

Moll, L. C., Amanti, C., Neff, D. and Gonzalez, N. (1992). 'Funds of knowledge for teaching: Using a qualitative approach to connect homes and classrooms', *Theory into Practice*, 31(2), pp. 132–41.

Murdick, N., Shore, P., Gartin, B. and Chittooran, M. M. (2004). 'Cross-cultural comparison of the concept of "otherness" and its impact on persons with disabilities', *Education and Training in Developmental Disabilities*, 39(4), pp. 310–16.

Norwich, B. (2002). 'Education, inclusion and individual differences: Recognising and resolving dilemmas', *British Journal of Educational Studies*, 50(4), pp. 482–502.

Prior, S. (2011). 'Student voice: What do students who are intellectually gifted say they experience and need in the inclusive classroom?', *Gifted and Talented International*, 26(1–2), pp. 121–9.

Prunty, A., Dupont, M. and McDaid, R. (2012). 'Voices of students with special educational needs (SEN): Views on schooling', *Support for Learning*, 27(1), pp. 29–36.

Sergeant, J. and Gillett-Swan, J. K. (2015). 'Empowering the disempowered through voice-inclusive practice: Children's views on adult-centric educational provision', *European Educational Research Journal*, 14(2), pp. 177–91.

Turnbull, A. P. and Turnbull, H. R. (2002). 'From the old to the new paradigm of disability and families: Research to enhance family quality of life outcomes', in James, L. P., Lavely, C. D., Cranston-Gringas, A., Taylor, E. L. (eds.) *Rethinking professional issues in special education*. Westport; London: Ablex Publishing, pp. 83–119.

United Nations General Assembly (1989). 'Convention on the Rights of the Child', General Assembly resolution, 44/25, 20 November. U.N. Doc. A/RES/44/25.

United Nations General Assembly (2006). 'Convention on the Rights of Persons with Disabilities', Resolution/Adopted by the General Assembly. A/RES/61/106.

Vigo-Arrazola, B. and Dieste-Gracia, B. (2019). 'Building virtual interaction spaces between family and school', *Ethnography and Education*, 14(2), pp. 206–22.

Wall, K., Cassidy, C., Robinson, C., Hall, E., Beaton, M., Kanyal, M. and Mitra, D. (2019). 'Look who's talking: Factors for considering the facilitation of very young children's voices', *Journal of Early Childhood Research*, 17(4), pp. 263–78.

Chapter 7 Working Together

Alsop, P. and Kupenga, T. R. (2016). *Mauri Ora: Wisdom from the Māori World*. New Zealand: Potton and Burton. Available at: https://www.pottonandburton.co.nz/ [as printed in]

Anning, A., Cottrell, D., Frost, N., Green, J. and Robinson, M. (2010). *Developing multi-professional teamwork for integrated children's services*. Maidenhead: Open University Press.

APPG Review (2012). *The All-Party Parliamentary Group for looked after children and care leavers*, APPG and UCU, Available at: http://dera.ioe.ac.uk/15782/1/Education_Matters_in_Care_September_2012.pdf

Bailey, R., Barrow, R., Carr, D. and McCarthy, C. (2013). *The SAGE handbook of philosophy of education*. London: Sage.

Corbett, J. and Slee, R. (2000). 'An international conversation on inclusive education', in Armstrong, F., Barton, L. and Armstrong, D. (eds.) *Inclusive education: Policy, contexts and comparative perspectives* (Vol.1:133–146). London: David Fulton.

Couper, C. (2019). 'Collaboration in the New Zealand School – Education Survey 2019' (Unpublished).

Cross, M. (2004). *Children with emotional and behavioural difficulties and communication problems*. London: Jessica Kingsley Publishers.

Department for Education and Department of Health (2014; 2015). *Special educational needs and disability code of practice: 0–25 years*, DfE. Available at: https://assets.publishing.service.gov.uk/government/uploads/system/uploads/attachment_data/file/398815/SEND_Code_of_Practice_January_2015.pdf

Glazzard, J. (2014). 'The standards agenda: reflections of a special educational needs co-ordinator', *Support for Learning*, 29(1), pp. 39–53.

Godemann, J. (2008). 'Knowledge integration: A key challenge for trans-disciplinary cooperation, *Environmental Education Research*, 14(6), pp. 625–41.

Gray, C. and Macblain, S. (2012). *Learning theories in childhood*. London: Sage.

Hutton, E. and Soan, S. (2015). '"Lessons Learned" from introducing universal strategies designed to support the motor and functional skills of Reception and Year 1 children in a sample of primary schools in South East England', *Education*, 3–13, pp. 1–21. doi:10.1080/03004279.2015.1048270

Kennedy, S. and Stewart, H. (2011). 'Collaboration between occupational therapists and teachers: Definitions, implementation and efficacy, *Australian Occupational Therapy Journal*, 58, pp. 209–14.

Lynch, S. L. and Irvine, A. N. (2009). 'Inclusive education and best practice for children with autism spectrum disorder: an integrated approach'. *International Journal of Inclusive Education*, 1(8), December, pp. 845–59.

Massey, A. (2016). *Provision mapping and the SEND code of practice*. 2nd edn. Abingdon: Routledge.

Nancarrow, S., Booth, A., Ariss, S., Smith, T., Enderby, P. and Roots, A. (2013). 'Ten principles of good interdisciplinary teamwork', *Human Resources for Health*, 11(19), pp. 1–11.

O'Toole, C. and Kirkpatrick, V. (2007). 'Building collaboration between professionals in health and education through interdisciplinary training, *Child Language Teaching and Therapy*, 23(3), pp. 325–52.

Salamanca Agreement United Nations Educational, Scientific and Cultural Organization (UNESCO) (1994). *The Salamanca statement and framework for action on special needs education*. Salamanca: UNESCO. Available at: www.unesco.org/education.pdf/SALAMA_E.PDF

Soan, S. (2013). *An exploration through a small number of case studies of the education provision for looked after children who have experienced early life abuse or neglect* (Unpublished PhD). The University of Kent/CCCU.

Soan, S. (2019). 'Multi-disciplinary practice and inclusive education', in Schuelka, M. J., Johnstone, C. J., Thomas, G. and Artiles, A. J. (eds.) *The SAGE handbook of inclusion and diversity in education*. London: Sage, pp. 307–21.

UNICEF (1989). *The UN convention on the rights of the child*. Available at: https://www.unicef.org/child-rights-convention/what-is-the-convention

United Nations Educational, Scientific and Cultural Organization (UNESCO) (2000). *The Dakar Framework for Action. Education for All: Meeting our collective commitments*. Paris: UNESCO.

Chapter 8 Resilience, Reflection and Reflexivity

Beltman, S. (2015). 'Teacher professional resilience: Thriving not just surviving', in Weatherby-Fell, N. (ed.) *Learning to teach in the secondary school*. Melbourne, Australia: Cambridge University Press, pp. 20–38.

Bolton, G. and Delderfield, R. (2018). *Reflective practice: Writing and professional development*. 5th edn. London: Sage.

Booth, T. and Ainscow, M. (2011). *Index for inclusion, developing learning and participation in schools*. Bristol: Centre for Studies on Inclusive Education.

Booth, T. and Ainscow, M. (2016). *Index for inclusion: A guide to school development led by inclusive values*. 4th edn. Cambridge: Index for Inclusion Network.

Boud, D., Keogh, R. and Walker, D. (1985). *Reflection: Turning experience into learning*. Abingdon: RougledgeFalmer.

Bourdieu, P. with Wacquant, L. (1992). *An invitation to reflexive sociology*. Translated by Wacquant, L. Oxford: Polity.

Charles, S. (2019). 'Dyslexia spells trouble: Disclosure and discrimination within the UK primary teaching profession', in Chiou, V., Holz, O., Oruç Ertürk, N. and Shelton, F. (eds.) *International insights: Equality in education*. Munster Germany: Waxman.

Claxton, G. (2018). 'Deep rivers of learning: Get below surface-level knowledge to help students build attitudes and habits that will stay with them for a lifetime', *Phi Delta Kappan*, 99(6), pp. 45–8.

Dall'Alba, G. (2009). 'Learning professional ways of being: Ambiguities of becoming', in Dall'Alba, G. (ed.) *Exploring education through phenomenology*. Oxford and Malden, MA: Wiley-Blackwell, pp. 41–52.

Day, C. (2017). *Teachers' worlds and work: Understanding complexity, building quality*. Abingdon: Routledge.

Day, C. and Gu, Q. (2014). 'Response to Margolis, Hodge and Alexandrou: Misrepresentations of teacher resilience and hope', *Journal of Education for Research*, 40(4), pp. 409–12.

Department for Education (2014). *The national curriculum in England: Framework document*. Available at: https://www.gov.uk/government/publications/national-curriculum-in-england-framework-for-key-stages-1-to-4

Dewey, J. (1933). *How we think: A restatement of the relation of reflective thinking in the educative process*. Boston, MA: DC Health & Co.

Dweck, C. (2015). *A Joosr guide to mindset: The new psychology of success*. Citheroe: Bookish.

Eraut, M. (1995). 'Schon Shock: A case for reframing reflection in action', *Teachers and Teaching*, 1, pp. 9–22.

Gadamer, H. (1998). *The relevance of the beautiful and other essays*, in Walker, N. and Bernasconi, R. (eds.) Cambridge: Cambridge University Press (Original work published 1986).

Gray, G., Wilcox, G. and Nordstokke, D. (2017). 'Teacher mental health, school climate, inclusive education and student learning: A review', *Canadian Psychology*, 58(3), pp. 203–10.

Helsing, D. (2007). 'Regarding uncertainty in teachers and teaching', *Teaching and Teacher Education*, 23(8), pp. 1317–33.

Hilton, J. (2018). *Ten traits of resilience*. London: Bloomsbury.

Hodkinson, A. (2016). *Key issues in special educational needs and inclusion*. 2nd edn. London: Sage.

Howard, S. and Johnson, B. (2004). 'Resilient teachers: Resisting stress and burnout', *Social Psychology of Education*, 7(4), pp. 399–420.

Hymer, B. and Michel, D. (2002). *Gifted and talented learners: Creating a policy for inclusion*. Abingdon: David Fulton.

Jordan, A., Schwartz, E. and McGhie-Richmond, B. (2009). 'Preparing teachers for inclusive classrooms', *Teaching and Teacher Education*, 25, pp. 535–42.

Kennedy, M. (2010). 'Attribution error and the question for teacher quality', *Educational Researcher*, 39(8), pp. 591–8.

Kroll, L. (2012). *Self study and inquiry into practice: Learning to teach for equality and social justice in the elementary school classroom*. Abingdon: Routledge.

Lambe, J. and Bones, R. (2007). 'The effect of school-based practice on student teachers' attitudes towards inclusive education in Northern Ireland', *Journal of Education for Teaching*, 33(1), pp. 99–131.

Margolis, J. and Alexandrou, A. (2014). 'Reply to Professors Day and Qing Gu', *Journal of Education for Teaching*, 40(4), pp. 413–14.

Moltzen, R. (2006). 'Can "inclusion" work for the gifted and talented?', in Smith, C. (ed.) *Including the gifted and talented: Making inclusion work for more gifted and able learners*. Abingdon: Routledge, pp. 41–55.

Moltzen, R. (2011). 'Inclusive education and gifted and talented provision', in Richards, G. and Armstrong, F. (eds.) *Teaching and learning in diverse and inclusive classrooms*. Abingdon: Routledge, pp. 102–12.

Norwich, B. and Ylonen, A. (2014). 'Lesson study practices in the development of secondary teaching of students with moderate learning difficulties: A systematic qualitative analysis in relation to context and outcomes', *British Educational Research Journal*, 41(4), pp. 629–49.

Oliver, M. (2004). 'If I had a hammer: The social model in action', in Swain, J., French, S., Barnes, C. and Thomas, C. (eds.) *Disabling barriers enabling environments*. London: Sage, pp. 7–12.

Robinson, D. (2017). 'Developing the effectiveness of teacher education for inclusion'. Presented at the Global Conference of Education Research, University of South Florida, Sarasota-Manatee, FL, USA, 22–25 May.

Schön, D. (1983). *The reflective practitioner*. San Francisco, CA: Jossey-Bass.

Sellars, M. (2017). *Reflective practice for teachers*. 2nd edn. London: Sage.

Silverman, L. (2019). 'Hidden treasures: Twice exceptional students', in Wallace, B., Sisk, A. and Senior, J. (eds.) *The Sage handbook of gifted and talented education*. London: Sage, pp. 144–58.

Sternberg, R. (2019). 'Is gifted education on the right path?' in Wallace, B., Sisk, A. and Senior, J. (eds.) *The Sage handbook of gifted and talented education*. London: Sage, pp. 5–18.

Ungar, M. (2012). 'Social ecologies and their contribution to resilience', in Ungar, M. (ed.) *The socialecology ofresilience: A handbook of theory and practice*. New York; Heidelberg; Dordrecht; London: Springer.

van Manen, M. (1990). *Researching the lived experience, human science for an action sensitive pedagogy*. New York: The State University Press.

Vygotsky, L. (1962). *Thought and language*. New York: Wiley.

Wharton, J., Codina, G., Middleton, T. and Esposito, R. (2019). *SENCO induction pack: Supporting you at the start of your journey*. Whole School SEND/DfE/LLSENDCiC/ nasen. Available at: https://www.sendgateway.org.uk/whole-school-send/sencos-area/ (accessed 2 August 2019).

Chapter 9 The Role of Teachers and Teaching

Armstrong, D. and Squires, G. (eds.) (2012). *Contemporary issues in special educational needs: Considering the whole child*. Maidenhead: OUP.

Barned, N. E., Flanagan Knapp, N. and Neuharth-Pritchett, S. (2011). 'Knowledge and attitudes of early childhood preservice teachers regarding the inclusion of children with autism spectrum disorder', *Journal of Early Childhood Teacher Education*, 32(4), pp. 302–21. doi:10.1080/10901027.2011.622235

Booth, T. and Ainscow, M. (2011). *Index for inclusion: Developing learning and participation inschools*. Bristol: Centre for Studies on Inclusive Education.

Caplan, B., Feldman, M., Eisenhower, A. and Blacher, J. (2016). 'Student-teacher relationships for young children with Autism Spectrum Disorder: Risk and protective factors', *Journal of Autism and Developmental Disorders*, 46, pp. 3653–66. doi: 10.1007/s10803-016-2915-1

Department for Education (2011). *National Teachers' Standards*. Available at: https://assets.publishing.service.gov.uk/government/uploads/system/uploads/attachment_data/file/665520/Teachers__Standards.pdf

Department for Education (2013). 'Achievement for All: Effect on SEND pupils', DfE.

Department for Education and Department of Health (2015). *The special educational needs and disability code of practice: 0–25 years*. DfE.

Ekins, A. (2012). *The changing face of special educational needs*. London: Routledge.

Foster, D. (2018). *Teacher recruitment and retention in England*, Briefing Paper No. 72222, December. Available at: http://researchbriefings.files.parliament.uk/documents/CBP-7222/CBP-7222.pdf

Gu, Q. (2014). 'How do people become effective teachers?', in Pollard, A. (ed.) *Readings for reflective teaching in schools*. 2nd edn. London: Bloomsbury, pp. 4–6.

Hattie, J. (2016). *Third visible learning annual conference: Mindframes and maximizers*. Washington, DC, 11 July. Available at: https://visible-learning.org/2018/03/collective-teacher-efficacy-hattie/

Huskin, P. R., Reiser-Robbins, C. and Kwon, S. (2018). 'Attitudes of undergraduate students toward persons with disabilities: Exploring effects of contact experience on social distance across ten disability types', *Rehabilitation Counseling Bulletin*, 62(1), pp. 53–63.

Lindblom, A., Dindar, K., Soan, S., Kärnä, E., Roos, C. and Carew, M. T. (2020). 'Predictors and mediators of European student teacher attitudes toward autism spectrum disorder', *Teaching and Teacher Education*, 89(102993), pp. 1–10.

Montgomery, D. (ed.) (2009). *Able, gifted and talented underachievers.* 2nd edn. Chichester: John Wiley and Sons Ltd.

O'Reilly, N. (2016). 'The key components to creating effective collaborative teaching and learning environments', Thesis Publication University of Canterbury, New Zealand. Available at: https://ir.canterbury.ac.nz/handle/10092/12190

Pillen, M. T., Den Brock, P. J. and Beijard, D. (2013). 'Profiles and change in beginning teachers' professional identity tensions', *Teaching and Teacher Education,* 34, pp. 86–97.

Reid, A. (2010). 'The politics of educational change', in Arthur, J. and Davies, I. (eds.) *Education studies textbook,* Abingdon: Routledge.

Sachs, J. (2016). 'Teacher Professionalism, why are we still talking about it?', *Teachers and Teaching: Theory and Practice,* 22(4), pp. 413–25.

White, D., Hillier, A., Frye, A. and Makrez, E. (2016). 'College students' knowledge and attitudes towards students on the autism spectrum', *Journal of Autism and Developmental Disorders.* Advance online publication. doi:10.1007/s10803-016-2818-1.

Wood, R. and Jackson, C. (2020). 'The important role of the teacher', Chapter 9, in Campbell-Barr, V. and Maisey, D. (eds.) *Why do teachers need to know about child development.* London: Bloomsbury.

Index

Boldface locators indicate figures and tables; locators followed by "n." indicate endnotes